First-Person Messiah

Transforming Your Life through Amazing Encounters with Jesus

STEPHEN K. MOORE

WESTBOW
PRESS®
A DIVISION OF THOMAS NELSON
& ZONDERVAN

This book is a work of non-fiction. Unless otherwise noted, the author and the publisher make no explicit guarantees as to the accuracy of the information contained in this book and in some cases, names of people and places have been altered to protect their privacy.

WestBow Press books may be ordered through booksellers or by contacting:

WestBow Press
A Division of Thomas Nelson & Zondervan
1663 Liberty Drive
Bloomington, IN 47403
www.westbowpress.com
844-714-3454

Because of the dynamic nature of the Internet, any web addresses or links contained in this book may have changed since publication and may no longer be valid. The views expressed in this work are solely those of the author and do not necessarily reflect the views of the publisher, and the publisher hereby disclaims any responsibility for them.

Any people depicted in stock imagery provided by Getty Images are models, and such images are being used for illustrative purposes only. Certain stock imagery © Getty Images.

Unless otherwise indicated, scripture quotations are from the ESV Bible® (The Holy Bible, English Standard Version®), copyright © 2001 by Crossway Bibles, a publishing ministry of Good News Publishers. Used by permission. All rights reserved.

Scripture quotations marked NIV are taken from the Holy Bible, New International Version®, NIV®. Copyright © 1973, 1978, 1984 by Biblica, Inc.™ Used by permission of Zondervan. All rights reserved worldwide.

Scripture quotations marked NLT are taken from the Holy Bible, New Living Translation, copyright © 1996, 2004, 2007 by Tyndale House Foundation. Used by permission of Tyndale House Publishers, Inc., Carol Stream, Illinois 60188. All rights reserved.

ISBN: 978-1-9736-9954-5 (sc)
ISBN: 978-1-9736-9955-2 (hc)
ISBN: 978-1-9736-9956-9 (e)

Library of Congress Control Number: 2023909901

Print information available on the last page.

WestBow Press rev. date: 08/11/2023

CONTENTS

Introduction

THE DEATH OF IMAGINATION

The Need for First-Person Messiah

A GOOD FRIEND OF MINE TOOK HIS WIFE TO A WAR MOVIE, THEY bought a big bucket of popcorn and a couple of sodas and sat down near the front. The movie opened with its first scene; his wife had just put her hand into the bucket for her first munchies. The scene was so intense that she withdrew her hand, put it over her mouth in shock, and it pretty much stayed there for the first thirty minutes of the show.

My friend, a true foody with a high metabolism, finished the whole bucket before her hand returned to the popcorn.

If you were to compare the movies of today, such as the ones my good friends went to, to the great movies of old, the difference is stunning.

Case in point, the old war movies start gradually, usually with an introduction to the various main characters, a crisis situation, and a slowly building tension toward the final climactic victory.

In the words of my young friends, the movies of old are boring. The new movies hook your attention nearly instantly and continue to stoke your emotions strongly and at irregular intervals throughout.

For that matter, all of our life today, with on-demand streaming videos on our smartphones, high-resolution video games with networking capability, and the huge high-definition televisions with a nearly limitless number of streaming channels, life is just a whole lot more exciting than it was when I was a kid.

It is also mostly brain-dead.

Our always-on, very intense video media culture bathes our minds in images, sound, and music and causes a continual flow of the brain chemical dopamine; our brains are completely passive while engaging these episodes of amusement.

Amusement comes from two old words meaning "without" and "the mind."

Yep, brain-dead.

If we receive too much of this exciting yet mindless input, our imagination, our ability to create with the mind, dies.

That is, if we ever developed our imagination at all.

When I assign Bible reading to adults and teens alike, very few do the assignment; most admit they don't think they can. My friends say they cannot get anything from the text, they cannot seem to devote any time to it, or they fall asleep.

WHAT WE HAVE LOST

I grew up with a black-and-white TV set that received three-and-a-half channels through an antenna on the roof of our house. Some days, the picture would be almost gone, and my mom would send me out to the back of the house with some tape—because it was the sign that our dog had partially chewed through the antenna wire. I suppose we weren't feeding him enough.

Games were board games; we owned maybe five games, plus a deck of cards, and some dominos. We lived pretty much paycheck-to-paycheck and didn't have a lot of extra money to go out to eat or shop.

What did we do for fun, as kids? (This is important to who we are as adults, I promise you.) We read books. Mom often said, "Get in the car, we are going to the library." I was a typical kid and often resisted my mom's ideas. But I never delayed going to the car for a trip to the library.

The library, even in our small town, was exciting. Even I, as a young boy, could check out books and bring them home to read.

Sounds dull in this age. That's because as a society, we have let our imaginations atrophy; our attention span is nearly nonexistent, and our empathic reading abilities died or were never developed.

I see in too many people today what I term *a-literacy.* The "a" means "without" and literacy conveys "competency in understanding."

When I work with kids or adults today and ask them to read a passage of scripture, they can decode the squiggles on the page into sound relatively well.

The problem is, and this is huge, when I ask them what it means, I often get silence.

They cannot make meaning out of what they read.

It gets worse.

SWEATING WHILE READING

I was preparing a Bible class recently on the sayings of Jesus to his followers as he moved toward his Crucifixion and departure. The whole flow of words started with his big saying of "Follow me," and they did. As time went on, he urged them to learn to walk in the Spirit and also started telling them that at some point, he would die and return to the Father above.

They couldn't hear it.

But finally, he tells them he is leaving and they cannot follow him.

As I read this, and some of the things he said shortly thereafter, I found my pulse elevated, and I was sweating.

Sweating while reading the Gospel of John?

Yep, that's because of my past reading experiences.

When I read, I do what I have come to call *empathic reading.* I put myself in the story.

This comes from the boring days of my youth.

I wanted to fly airplanes, and so I read a lot of stories written by and about those people who flew—mostly in wartime. I learned these people were people just like me; in spite of their brave smiling faces in the pictures, they were actually scared and doing amazing things simply out of grit and a conviction their cause was just. Many of them ended up having what was called "shell-shock," a nervous breakdown, and this confused me, but as I struggled to understand, I learned empathy; just as certain things in my young life terrified me (such as singing in front of people or talking to a pretty girl), these guys were for some reason afraid of these aircraft they barely knew how to fly and the bullets and flak that regularly ripped through the thin aluminum aircraft and killed people.

Go figure.

In my mind, I slowly learned to be there with them. I wasn't just decoding squiggles into internal sounds; those squiggles activated a 3-D surround-sound movie in my brain. I could hear the cannon of the aircraft, feel the buffeting of the flak explosions around me, and feel the acceleration of the aircraft as I jammed the throttle forward to chase an enemy plane. I began tasting the fear in my mouth, something that would come back to me decades later when I began flying combat missions.

Not bad for a skinny twelve-year-old nerd who had never left the ground.

Jumping forward almost fifty years, I still read the same way, only more so. When I'm reading John chapter 13 and the God-man who I am thinking is the Messiah, who healed me of blindness, and who I have been literally following, when he suddenly says, "Where I am going you cannot come,"[1] I am seeing him, my heart is racing, and I suddenly understand the intense sadness, confusion, and disappointment all the disciples must have felt that day. It makes my mind race and drives me to seek everything else he had told his closest followers up to this point. I am trying to understand how to follow Jesus now through understanding what those first believers experienced then.

The story of Jesus is intense. His history is grueling, awe-inspiring, and spiritually sustaining.

And too many of us today get nothing from it, spend no time in the Word, or fall asleep.

We miss seeing the beauty, the tension, the confusion, and the great joy of walking with Jesus—what we should be seeing when

---

[1] John 13:33.

we open our Bibles and sit with the Spirit and experience our Lord through the Word.

We need to reclaim the mental capabilities our Creator gave us and see Jesus in all of his beauty.

THE FIRST-PERSON EMPATHIC VIEW OF YESHUA

That is why this book exists.

This started as what I call an "audible" by the Holy Spirit.

I was leading a new class at church called *Seeing Jesus, Walking With.*

I had a lesson prepared about reading the Bible empathically, with all the merits described as to why the class members should do so.

But the Sunday morning of the class, I awoke early (I have a standing request of the Lord to wake me up when he needs to get up in order to teach me something [I lose a lot of sleep this way]), and the Spirit gave me new orders for the day.

I was led to ditch the lesson I had prepared and instead show the beauty of who Jesus was and the power of empathic reading by writing the story of the "Woman at the Well" found in John chapter 4 as a first-person experience; that is, let the class see Jesus through the eyes of the Samaritan woman.

To be honest, it seemed risky and a bit edgy for what our class was usually like, but hey, the Spirit woke me up; it was his idea. I supposed if it flopped, I could blame him.

So for two hours I wrote furiously, then I went to meet with our church family and simply read the first-person story as written.

It was amazing.

As a teacher, I can always tell when what I am saying is hitting home, and on this morning, the view of Jesus from the imagined (Spirit-led?) but powerful perspective of a despised woman who had been married five times and was now just shacking up; well, it was resonating big time.

I saw many tears, I saw intense eye contact, and the comments afterwards let me know that the early wakeup was indeed of the Spirit.

And thus, this book was born; the goal of this genre I call Empathic Biblical Historical Fiction is to assist those who perhaps are lacking in the ability to place themselves in a historical narrative. My prayer is that this simple work will help everyone approach the Bible and all history with a new level of excitement and transformation.

My hope is that each morning after you read this, you will be awakened by the Spirit to sit with him in a comfortable spot, maybe with coffee, and to receive sweaty armpits and a rapidly beating heart as you walk alongside God and his people in the most amazing and powerful story ever told.

As you come along with me through my imagination of these events, may you learn how to do exactly what I have done here. I promise that if you do, you will find yourself curled up in a comfy chair, enjoying the Bible and other great works of literature as a preferred means of the path to peace, understanding, and wisdom.

OBJECTIONS UNDERSTOOD

I know we are not to add or take away from the inspired Word, and thus I do want to stress that this is historical fiction with a purpose.

I am a someone who loves the backstories.

I find every person fascinating; I love listening to people even if they think themselves to be boring.

But the Bible was written in a time when writing was difficult. Ink and writing surfaces were precious, and reproducing works was slow and tedious. One person could make one copy at a time, at a very slow pace. What was recorded was recorded very succinctly, often with no backstory.

As a result, the Bible says a lot in a very little space.

When we read the story of Mary, there are so many questions that come to mind. But very little is said of the internal struggles she went through, or of conflict with her family over her sudden pregnancy, or any other of the stress-filled consequences of an unmarried teenager who finds herself pregnant.

Why was Nicodemus so receptive to this Nazarene rabbi being the Messiah when so many of his fellow Pharisees (Phellow Pharisees?) were not?

Why was the apostle Thomas so hesitant to believe things he could not touch?

Why was Mary of "Mary, Martha, and Lazarus," so unaware of her expected duties as a woman in Hebrew culture? What was it like to a friend of Jesus who irritated Martha so much?

The purpose of this writing is to use our God-given imagination to supply some possibilities of the backstory, to help us understand the cultural issues of the day, and to relate the struggles of the time to our own. The big purpose is to help us see and love the amazing rabbi from Nazareth in a fresh and transformative way.

Every attempt is made to not change anything of substance about the teachings or the person of Christ. Some historical and cultural background is woven into the narrative of the characters to help better understand the challenges of the times of Jesus. I highly encourage you to read the biblical story to firmly know what is true, and what is the fictional enhancement.

At the same time, the language is mostly modern—to make the whole of this experience accessible to all. I have attempted to select reasonable Hebrew names for those the scripture does not name.

I would suggest this goal if you read this book—learn to engage in reading in the way this old guy did as a kid in a more boring time. Many child psychologists are commending the value of boredom to the development of a child's creative capabilities and attention span. Embrace times of boredom, put your devices away from you, and put yourself in the amazing and wondrous story of the rabbi from Nazareth. Learn to read empathically. Learn to read scripture, especially the historical sections, by seeing them in your head.

Research has shown that when you engage in deep reading (undistracted and totally focused reading during which you are unaware of time or what is happening around you), the parts of your brain that would activate if you were actually in the situation you are reading about, actually activate.

In other words, you can do more than just acquire information about the Savior of the world.

You. Can. Experience. Him.

Read on, empathically.

Chapter One

YOU SHALL SEE THE CHRIST
Old Simeon's Joy

I OPENED MY EYES. IT HAD BEEN A FITFUL NIGHT OF SLEEP. Nothing terribly unusual in that. It seemed the older I got, the more I perceived I needed to sleep, and the less I could do so.

It was still dark, or mostly dark. I pushed myself up from my pallet. It was cold, and my body was aching. Being old was not fun—well, maybe sometimes it was.

I lived with my son and his family, and getting to be with his children was my excuse to act like a child. Everyone thought me gracious to play with the kids, but it was really just good fun. I enjoyed their company, their appreciation for the small things, and laughing with them made my aching body feel younger.

I looked around in the dim light. My son, Yechezkel, was sleeping with his wife just through the door to the other room. The kids were next to me. I could see through the window the eastern sky just beginning to glow.

I lay back down. My bones were really hurting.

I quieted my mind and started my usual conversation. "Lord, you are glorious. It is so good to be with you. Thank you for making me welcomed and loved in my son's house."

I thought back over the past few weeks; much was happening between the Lord and me.

"Where is the Lord?" was the question my people asked.

To be honest, it used to be my question too.

But no more.

I listened. It was getting harder to do sometimes. Like this morning, when the cold of the morning made my joints hurt more than usual, and it was harder to breathe—well, it was harder to do anything, or do nothing.

But I quieted myself. I listened.

"The temple." The image of the temple came to me, and I suddenly was intrigued. But there was something more, something odd. I perceived a brief image of a young couple. Husband and wife? I didn't know. The man seemed a little older; was he her father? He wasn't very impressive looking; he looked like a regular hard-working neighbor. Was the unimpressive-looking man the Messiah?

"He had no form or majesty that we should look at him, and no beauty that we should desire him." That was what the prophet Isaiah had foretold about the coming Messiah.[2] Curious. Was this the suffering servant? The thought excited me.

The pain in my body broke through my thoughts. There was no need to rest anymore. Rest was just impossible some mornings. This morning.

---

[2] Isaiah 53:2 (ESV).

"No need to understand, my Lord. To the temple I go."

I sat up suddenly, then I rose to my feet. I laughed loudly, always joyous that the Lord would speak to someone like me.

My son heard me get up, stirred, and asked, "Abba, you OK?"

"Shalom, my son. I'm very OK. Shalom."

I grabbed my tunic and pulled it over my head (with difficulty, of course) and wrapped the tie around me. I laughed again.

I had reached that age when I made a noise every time I moved. For some reason, it struck me as funny, and I laughed. Laughing felt good. It sort of canceled out the pain. I desired to be quiet so as not to wake the kids, but I could not silence my groaning.

Laughing calmed the anguish in my heart over Israel. She was in bad shape. "Lord, is today the day you will redeem Israel?"

The temple flashed into my head again. Yes, I must go to the temple. Perhaps today would be the day when he arrived.

I tried to straighten myself a bit, but nothing on me was straight anymore. I laughed out loud as I looked down at my crooked and bony body.

Yechezkel heard me again and propped himself up for a moment. "Abba, where are you going? Sleep a while longer."

"Son, the Lord is sending me to the temple; you should come with me."

"The temple will be there after breakfast too. Rest longer, and then let Sara get you something to eat. You need your rest, Abba."

"I am very full, my son. I cannot rest. Something is happening at the temple today; you should come with me."

"Hearing from God again?"

My son was a wonderful man, but he thought I was losing my mind. I suppose everyone who knew me thought the same.

"Why is God silent?" they all asked. And then when someone heard from him, they made fun of the person.

A silent God? The one who made us all and all there is? Why was he silent?

He wasn't. He couldn't be.

"Shalom, my son. Shalom. Sleep on."

The Lord was patient with us all, and I must be patient with my son. He was busy being a husband, a father, and a shepherd. Faith was a growing thing, like a tree. We could not become mighty overnight. I prayed my son would grow to know the joy of hearing and seeing the Lord.

I pushed through the door and started toward the temple.

I had come to perceive that the Lord had never been silent, but he was not rude. The proud voice in our heads was usually louder than his; it was his gentle way. We were too busy worrying about every little thing in life—and trying to be in charge of life. But if we would quiet ourselves and seek the Lord, he would give us what we needed. And we would hear his voice.

If we let him run the show, we would see he always knew better than we did and would lead us into the good things.

One best encountered the voice of the Lord gently at first, to test it. As King David said, we must "taste and see that the LORD is good."

I never heard him at all until life silenced me. When my jewel, my sweet Miriam, when she gave her all to give me my Yechezkel. He lived; she didn't. She was only a girl. Twenty years old, beautiful, smart, and loving. She was the best wife, best mom, best friend—everything. She was my comfort, my rock.

And she turned ghostly white as her blood ran out of her as I held Yechezkel in my arms for the first time, maybe two minutes after he was born.

I was lost for a long time. Angry—violently angry. I would shake my fist at God and call him the worst. It was a very ugly and hopeless season of life.

But then for some reason, I gave up. I got tired of crying, and I grew quiet. I raised my two sons. I tried to smile for them. It was a fake smile, except when they made me laugh. I took them to the temple several times a week. Everyone praised me for my faithfulness. I wasn't faithful; I was just numb and didn't know what else to do.

I only went to the temple because the people there helped my kids. It was just practical, not spiritual. They cared for, clothed, and fed my kids when I didn't care to.

I just couldn't find the energy to do much of anything except survive.

Then Yechezkel lost his favorite dog when he was six. She was in the field with the sheep. An animal attacked the sheep, and she died trying to do what she was made to do.

Yechezkel was hurt and furious, much as I had been when Miriam died.

His grief and tears awoke me from my numbness. He had always been the happiest boy, even smiling as a tiny baby. His laughter kept me going, and he wasn't laughing anymore. I needed my boy to smile again.

One day, when I was trying to comfort him, I heard myself tell him earnestly, "My son, your dog was doing what dogs do. She loved her sheep, and she died so they could live. She couldn't have done anything else. That was her way of love. It is the way life is."

My son stared straight ahead for a while. I could tell he was thinking. Then he looked into my eyes, tears streaming from his, and he smiled. "You are right, Abba. God is good. He gave me the dog for a while, but she had something she had to do. I must be thankful for the time that I knew her. She loved those sheep, and she was doing what she had to do." He looked thoughtful again and then said, "Just like my mother; she did what she had to do to give me to you." He turned his head, still staring into my face. "Why are you crying, Abba?"

I felt tears rolling down my face. They were not angry tears as I had experienced when Miriam died; they felt good. Years of anger were washing away.

I was confused. The words I had said to my boy, they had just come. I hadn't thought them through; they'd just flowed through me as if someone had poured them into an opening in my head, and straight out of my mouth they went.

And they had soothed my little boy's grief. He'd figured it out and turned my words back on me.

His words had finished my grief.

But they didn't seem to be my words. I wondered if the Spirit of God was speaking through both of us that day.

My boy stared into my face. I reached down, picked him up, and squeezed him tight.

"Yes, my wise son, God is good all the time. He gave us the good dog and your beautiful mom, who gave me you. This is the way she loves us. This is the way God loves us." We cried together for a long time.

I was back with God, but he had never left me.

He spoke through me in the midst of my unbelief.

No, God was never silent; we just refused to be quiet and listen. Or when he did speak, we claimed it as our own wisdom.

I looked at the houses and shops as I walked on. If only my people could be quiet enough to hear. Our Lord was always here; yes, was the Messiah coming here today?

Today, maybe this is the day. Of course, my son thinks I've lost my mind; he awaits the Messiah like all of my people. But he waits for the figure of David: a king returning from battle, noble and handsome. That is the way man rules the world. A man who can lead armies to hack into the enemy and defend the land.

But what of that young couple I saw—what if that man is the Messiah? He isn't very like David, at least as I perceive him. Will my people accept a Messiah who isn't riding into town like a conquering hero?

I worried. I hadn't thought about it; no one wanted to hear what I was hearing from the Lord. They thought I was losing my grip on reality. If this young, ordinary-looking Jew is the Messiah, will anyone accept him?

"He was despised and rejected by men"; yes, it would be okay. Isaiah had given us the Word from the Lord. Some would reject him. But the Messiah would be triumphant in his mission.

How long had it been? Six, seven years since I heard God say, "You will see the anointed one before I bring you home."[3]

It was stunning, exciting, and I tried to share it with my son and his family; I could see the fear in their eyes. I could almost hear their thoughts, *The old man is getting loony.* But he did ask me, "Do you hear a real voice? What does God sound like?"

---

[3] Luke 2:26, paraphrased.

It isn't like that; it is more like a very strong impression, someone communicating within me but without sound. Could I be wrong? Sure. But my Lord taught me to hear.

Would this ordinary man standing with an ordinary woman, would this be the arrival of the salvation of Israel and the world? Would he arrive so humbly, so beautifully, so unexpectedly?

"Where are you going so early, old man?"

I was startled back to my walk; I had lost track of where I was. In front of me were three Roman soldiers. The short one in the front was sneering at me; he had asked the question and now was right in my face, challenging me.

"To the temple, my son; where else does a Jew have to go when he is old?"

The other two guards laughed, but a quick glare from the leader silenced them.

"You better be careful, old man," he said, looking down at my legs and laughing. "It may be windy today, and you might be blown out of the city."

I looked at my legs, sticking awkwardly out from my old tunic. They were a sight. Once I was strong, and my legs were muscular and powerful and fast. I spent many years picking up sheep who had wandered down into a valley and hauling them on my shoulders to the crest again. In those days, I could have taken on this young soldier and likely taught him a lesson.

But now, my legs, well, I burst out laughing and said, "Yes, it looks like I borrowed the legs from my chicken this morning, and I shall fly away like a chicken too."

My tormentor broke, his laughter like a torrent of rain from a storm. He reached out to me and put his hand on my shoulder.

"You're okay, old man," he said, laughing. "You be careful in your flying."

"Shalom, my sons."

"Uh, yeah, shalom, good man," he said, somewhat awkwardly, looking very surprised that I would consider a Roman soldier my "son."

My good friends would be very disappointed in me. I had called Roman soldiers "sons." I would be on the bad list if they heard. We were the chosen of God. These Romans who ruled our land so harshly, they were the enemy.

But this morning, as on many other occasions, when I looked at these young men, they were no different than my own children. They were just far from home, being asked to subdue my people—and well, we were a difficult people. As the Lord had said through Isaiah, "I know that you are an obstinate people!"[4]

We are all, Roman, Syrian, Jew, or whoever, obstinate. And we are beautiful. I could still hear the soldiers behind me laughing and talking; they could be my sons. The Lord made us all, and he loves us all. They were good-looking boys, strong and scared, much like my own two.

Yes, my people had suffered much with the Romans. They took so much in taxes, they abused our daughters, and they harassed us continually.

But my people were sometimes faithless. We spoke of God, but too often, it was a god we had made in our own minds, a god that looked a lot like a weak Jewish man or woman. We made a big deal about the Temple, about Passover, and the Sabbath. We focus on

---

[4] Isaiah 48:4 NIV.

those things we can control and do in our own strength. And we make a mess of it all.

Oh my, the Sabbath. The day of rest had been turned into a day of tedious challenge by the Pharisees. Didn't God give us the commands, as Moses had said, for our own good? Shouldn't the Sabbath be a day we look forward to, find joy in, and be refreshed by? After all, Moses had said, "What does the LORD your God require of you, but to fear the LORD your God, to walk in all his ways, to love him, to serve the LORD your God with all your heart and with all your soul, and to keep the commandments and statutes of the LORD, which I am commanding you today for your good?"[5]

The Sabbath was supposed to be good, not a day of inconvenience and condemnation.

Shouldn't it be a day of community, laughter, and good food? Is this not how we enjoy the presence of God, by enjoying the greatest gift he gave us here: the love of his children made in his image?

I looked up; the temple was gleaming ahead of me. My breath was labored, but I did not care. The temple was glorious in the morning sun. The golden rays hit the white stone in such a way, it made you wonder what the heavenly kingdom of God was like if a temple in dusty Jerusalem could be this gorgeous.

I picked up the pace.

There had been many of us speaking of the Messiah lately. Many of my people just wanted someone to kick out the Romans, but some of us had something bigger in mind.

Of course, I had heard from the Spirit of God. I would not die before I saw him. And I was obviously on borrowed time already. I laughed out loud when I thought of it, as I looked again at my

---

[5] Deuteronomy 10:12.

withered legs and arms, and felt my lungs aching just to walk at what would have been a slow pace in my younger years. I saw movement to my right; a young woman had just swept some dust out of her door. She was watching me as I laughed to myself, and it made her smile.

"Shalom, sir! Happy today?"

"Shalom, my daughter. Messiah is coming, I think today, maybe?

Her face grimaced slightly, then she burst out laughing. "Well, yes, why not today? Enjoy the Messiah, Abba."

How sweet; either she agreed with my hope of the Messiah, or she was just being gracious to an old man. Most likely the latter. I'm happy, regardless.

Yes, Messiah was coming. Today? It had to be soon. I didn't have long left.

I wondered if Anna would be there today; yes, if the Spirit was speaking to me, he would be speaking to her. I would see her today.

She also had heard from the Lord on numerous occasions; many thought her more out of touch with reality than me. After all, she was "just a woman," as many would say amongst my people. How dare she suggest the Lord spoke to her and not to a man?

Anna was a great woman. Her husband had died much too soon when she was young. We had much in common.

I often mused about asking Anna to marry me, but the strange thing is, it just never seemed to be appropriate. As I watched her in the temple, she was clearly already spoken for. Her heart was given completely to the Lord. I learned how to pray by watching and listening to her. She was amazing; she seemed very content being married to the Lord.

When Anna would speak, I just listened. She was blessed with a wisdom that can only come from the Lord. Women are beautiful in their ability to trust and follow the Lord in ways we men in our stubborn pride seem to struggle to duplicate. She didn't seem to have that male need to prove everything possible the Lord had said; whatever he said was just good enough for her. She had a simple and trusting faith. I looked forward to hearing what Anna had heard when I saw her today.

I walked through the gates of the temple. A priest was kindling the fire. He looked up at me, and I said "Shalom."

"Umm, Shalom, Simeon, why are you here so early?" His voice was flat, and he seemed irritated.

"The Lord woke me. I believe Messiah is coming today."

He looked grim, shook his head, and went back to his fire. Why did the priests seem so angry most of the time? Shouldn't he be excited about the Messiah coming? Why do priests believe he is coming but that he is not coming today?

Interesting, the contrast between those evil Roman soldiers and the priest.

Both had some impressive-looking uniforms, but on the average, the Roman soldier had far more joy in living. They laughed more, and their community seemed to enjoy each other far more than the priests, scribes, and Pharisees.

Shouldn't those devoted to the Lord be the most joyful?

How could it be that possessing the precious scripture containing the Word and knowledge of our Lord would lead one to be so somber, critical, and downright mean? While the pagan soldiers enjoyed their friends, the blue sky, swimming, dancing, wine, and good food?

Shouldn't knowing the Lord, who made all things, bring a smile to one's face? Shouldn't someone who knows the Creator be unable to stop singing and dancing?

I sat down to rest on one of the benches in the outer court. I looked across the courtyard, and my eyes met Anna's. We both laughed; I waved and heard her shout, "Today, he is coming today."

The priest at the fire looked at her sternly; women are supposed to be seen and not heard, and preferably not seen much.

Anna and I burst out laughing; the priest threw down the last of his kindling and stormed off. Anna and I laughed even harder.

"Yes, my sister, today we shall see him."

A few more people were arriving in the outer court, and they were staring at us; laughter was not often heard in the temple; but shouldn't it be? If we are made in the image of God, and we like to laugh, aren't we just being like God?

I started looking at each person as they walked into the temple; I was hoping I would recognize the couple the Lord had shown me. The strain of life was showing on the faces of the adults, but the children were laughing and full of wonder. They enjoyed seeing the ornate decorations of the temple, while the adults didn't seem to look at them at all.

I saw a small girl staring upward at one of the majestic columns behind me, with its carved and gilded pomegranates and leaves at the top. I turned and looked too; they were beautiful, but as I looked back, she was far more amazingly crafted. Her face was so sweet, and in such a worshipful sense of joy. Why are we not happier and in awe of the beauty the Lord put all around us? We adults are anxious about far too many things; don't we know the Lord provides all for us? This precious little one didn't seem to be worried about what she would eat tomorrow, about the Roman taxes she would pay some day, or about her health. She was just enjoying the temple, in that moment, looking at every detail the craftsmen had spent so many decades producing.

As I enjoyed her upturned face, she suddenly sensed she was being watched, and she looked straight at me. I smiled, she smiled, and then a tear rolled down my face as I broke into a laugh.

She started running toward me, her mother yelling at her to stop, but she came and hopped into my lap and gave me a big hug.

"Are you sad?" she asked.

"Oh, no, my daughter; these are happy tears. The Lord made you so sweetly, I was just finding joy in your face."

She laughed. "Okay. So you are crying happy. That is very good."

"And I am pretty sure Messiah is coming today."

"He is? Please show him to me when he gets here." She laughed, and she jumped down and ran back to her mother.

Hmm, she didn't seem to think I was out of line; she just accepted the good news. She too had the simple trust that Anna does. Perhaps in my old age, I am a child once again. I just want to see Messiah too. I don't have to have everything figured out. So childish of me.

I saw the girl turn and look back at me as her parents walked away; she smiled and waved, but then, just past her, I saw them. My heart nearly stopped; it was them.

I found myself standing, walking; my eyes were fixed on the man. He was wiry, muscular, dark-skinned, but not particularly remarkable. He looked like any other Jewish working man.

We made eye contact; I think he was getting nervous, but I couldn't take my eyes off him. There "was nothing in his appearance" that gave me the impression of Messiah. This must be him. I was walking steadily toward him; he put his hand out and stopped the woman, and then he motioned toward me.

I was now face-to-face with the man; I studied him, and he apparently saw what I was thinking. He shook his head no and looked at the woman. I looked at her, and then I saw something else—no, someone else. She was holding a baby. I looked back at the man, and he nodded yes. I looked back to the baby, and then at the mother's face, my head tilted as if to ask, "Is this him?"

She smiled a beautiful smile; the tears were welling up in her eyes as they were in mine, and she nodded very rapidly in the affirmative.

A baby? The Messiah is a tiny baby? I had never even imagined.

I found my arms reaching for the child, and even more amazingly, the young mother smiled and handed him to me.

I hesitated. I was going to hold Messiah? No, I started to pull my arms back, but the girl, the mother, she stepped toward me and said, "Hold him; he is for all people."

I took him gently; he was so small and fragile. This was Messiah? A baby? How could this—

I felt my heart beating strong, like I was a young man again. I felt energetic and happy. I stared into this tiny face; he was beautiful, small, vulnerable, like every other baby I had ever held.

I looked back at the mother; she looked so young. The wrinkles of the cares of the world had not yet creased her skin. As I stared into her eyes, she blushed and looked at her child's face; she reached out, stroked his cheek, and whispered something. Her voice sounded unsure, as though she were struggling with what she said. I strained to listen, but I did hear it: "Immanuel."

God with us.

She knew and yet seemed unsure also. God coming through a young girl, as a baby; yes, it was so very hard to grasp.

Of course, his ways, well, like Isaiah said, "For as the heavens are higher than the earth, so are my ways higher than your ways and my thoughts than your thoughts."[6] I never dreamed, never even imagined, that the promised one would be a baby.

I felt as though I might pass out, and I thought I should hand the child back, but I wanted to hold him just a little longer. I knew my time was short, and now, this was the best moment of my life. Even better than holding my own children, even better than holding my precious Miriam.

The words of Isaiah came to me: "Behold, the virgin shall conceive and bear a son, and you shall call his name Immanuel."

She called him Immanuel.

God with us.

I was holding ... God.

And suddenly, it wasn't the first time, I heard my own voice speaking loudly; words poured through me from God's Spirit: "Sovereign Lord, now let your servant die in peace, as you have promised. I have seen your salvation, which you have prepared for all people. He is a light to reveal God to the nations, and he is the glory of your people Israel!"[7]

My tears were falling onto the face of Immanuel. I gently wiped them away, touching God? Yes, I was ready to die right on the spot.

---

[6] Isaiah 55:9.

[7] Luke 2:29–32 NLT.

Life here would never be better for me. I was holding my Lord. And he was holding my heart.

I pulled my eyes off the child for a moment; his parents looked dazed. A crowd had gathered around us; several of the priests and Pharisees were there. I had apparently been very loud for an old man.

I looked at all the faces; all were questioning, curious, confused. "This child is destined to cause many in Israel to fall, and many others to rise. He has been sent as a sign from God, but many will oppose him."[8] The words, they just came. It was the Spirit of God again. I looked; the chief priest was there. He looked angry enough to spit, undoubtedly at me.

He stared hard into my eyes and then muttered something under his breath; if I read his lips correctly, it was one word: "Blasphemy."

He turned away and stormed off; the other priest and several of the Pharisees quickly followed him to a corner and began talking urgently amongst themselves.

I heard my voice again: "The deepest thoughts of many hearts will be revealed."[9]

I thought to myself, *Isn't that the truth?* It was already happening. Those who should be the first to recognize the Christ were the first to walk away. What was in their hearts? Why would they not accept the Messiah coming as a baby? Isn't the Lord, God? Can he not come as he chooses?

I looked again at the couple. The man's hands were calloused; he was obviously a man who worked hard. Both of their clothes were fairly rough looking, a little dirty, a bit ragged; this couple was

---

[8] Ibid., v. 34.
[9] Ibid., v. 35.

poor. Did the Messiah come from the wrong parents as far as the priests were concerned?

The father in front of me might be a common laborer, but it was already clear the child would have to be a warrior. His time on earth would not be easy, if the people who should have been the first to worship were instead the first to reject.

I looked at the sweet mom; she was staring at the child again. I gently handed him back to her. I wrapped my arms around her and whispered in her ear, "Sweet daughter, a sword will pierce your very soul."[10]

As I pulled away, the young woman stared at me, looking very confused. I became aware of singing; it was Anna's voice, singing about this child and how he would redeem us all. But I sensed this woman was scared, unsure, and anxious. She wanted reassurance.

I looked at her; tears from both of us now rested on the child's face, and I heard myself say, "Shalom, my daughter," and I touched God one last time. "Rest in him; he is your Shalom."

I turned away; I could not monopolize the Savior any longer. I started the walk home; I felt as though I were floating. I had no more pain.

UNPACKING SIMEON

Very little is known about Simeon, but the reason he is included along with Anna in this story is because of what, or shall we say, who he was able to see and accept as he was. Here are a few takeaways for each of us from this story:

---

[10] Ibid.

BE HUMBLE IN YOUR FAITH

Even though we often give the priest, scribes, and Pharisees of Jesus's day a pretty hard time because of their rejection of Jesus, there is a critical lesson to be learned from them all; these folks put a lot of effort into their service of God. Many of them were in the scripture, they were public with their faith, and they generally were attempting to serve God in a most-correct manner.

And yet in spite of all their hard work, they failed to recognize the one scripture talks about from Genesis 3 onward.[11] This should be alarming to all who consider themselves to be followers of the Way.

We can be very sincere, be very diligent, and be in the company of other believers seeking to serve the Christ, and still completely miss him.

Think of Simeon and Anna in the temple, praising God and pronouncing that the baby of Mary and Joseph was the Messiah; they seem to have made quite a commotion, and yet apparently none of the priests really stopped to see who these folks were and investigate. There is no record of anyone giving serious consideration that Simeon and Anna had actually heard from God and that they were right in identifying the prophesied suffering servant as having arrived as a baby.

One part of the problem with so many of the priests and Pharisees was they were overconfident they had God all figured out. This is so tragic. This is not just a criticism leveled at them; it

---

[11] Genesis 3:15 is the first mention of the "seed of woman" (children were normally considered to be the "seed" of man) who would bruise the head of the serpent.

is true sorrow for their situation. So many of these men (and their wives, likely) who had much wider access to the sacred scripture that contained the numerous prophecies ended up standing side-by-side with the Messiah; not only did not recognize him, they fought against him.

They were missing that critical hard-learned lesson from the apostle Peter. He put it this way: "Clothe yourselves, all of you, with humility toward one another, for God opposes the proud but gives grace to the humble."[12]

Do you spend little time in the Word of God yet have strong opinions about what is right and wrong before him? If so, you are in danger of missing the outpouring of grace and power that both Simeon and Anna had the joy of experiencing.

Do not think too highly of yourself. Go before our great God and ask him to help you live this instruction from the apostle Paul: "Have this mind among yourselves, which is yours in Christ Jesus, who, though he was in the form of God, did not count equality with God a thing to be grasped, but emptied himself, by taking the form of a servant."[13]

> **TAKEAWAY 1:** Ask God to help you to be truly humble. Be willing to admit you are not all-knowing (i.e., that you are not God). Be open to correction, rebuke, and the gentle leading of the Spirit of God.

---

[12] 1 Peter 5:5.

[13] Philippians 2:5–7.

BEWARE OF SPIRITUAL GROUPTHINK

How do we know what we think is true is actually true?

I grew up in a faith tradition that was heavily legalistic and works-oriented. In our minds, and amongst ourselves (just as with the Pharisees), we had book, chapter, and verse from the Bible itself to justify why we were right and nearly everyone else was wrong. We (including myself in this group) were fully convinced of our rightness.

Much like the priests and Pharisees of Jesus's day, however, we in our church had inherited our doctrine from some well-intentioned but biased believers who went before us. We had been handed a system of belief strongly backed by certain verses in the Bible, and although we claimed we were open to being challenged, I pitied the person who ever did.

You see, the problem was that we were misusing scripture.

This problem is still very common today, to the point that catechisms, creeds, statements of beliefs, and even Bible commentaries often enable the continuing abuse of scripture.

It is vital that we combine the humility mentioned above (i.e., admitting that much of what we know has been handed to us) with an admission that there is nearly always pressure from our type of church family (whether conservative, community, orthodox, Catholic, charismatic, or whatever) to embrace what is taught—mostly without questioning it.

We may say we are open to questions, but are we really?

How different would the scene at the temple have been, with Simeon, Anna, Mary, Joseph, and the baby Savior, if the priests on duty had heard what Simeon and Anna had proclaimed, asked Mary and Joseph a few questions, and then gone to examine the scrolls (especially Isaiah) and asked themselves, "Could this be the Messiah?"

You see, many were expecting a heroic figure like King David, or another religious leader like one of Maccabees,[14] to deliver the nation of Israel from their captors and establish an earthly sovereign kingdom.

But if they had only understood the nature of the social pressure put upon us by even our best God-fearing friends, imagine the possibilities.

That being said, be humble and understand the deadly influence of religious groupthink. Understand that no matter how strongly you believe your system of faith is right, ultimately, we are not saved by a system. Understand that most of us do not actually think well. If you are not convicted of this, I highly recommend the amazing book *Thinking, Fast and Slow* by Daniel Kahneman.[15] The big point in this book is what is illustrated in the story of Simeon, Anna, and all of the Temple staff. The baby Simeon and Anna praised and accepted was and is the Messiah. Because of the groupthink and non-thinking nature of those who should have been the first to recognize the Savior, they missed him. We must humbly realize our tendency to not think and not be humble.

> **TAKEAWAY 2:** In whatever spiritual circles you run, realize we may adopt attitudes and beliefs about God that are wrong. Be willing to listen to others, and learn to ask yourself, "How do I know what I think I know?"

---

[14] Judas Maccabeus was the son of a Jewish priest who led a revolt against the Selucid occupiers and reestablished the national sovereignty of Judea for a time.

[15] Daniel Kahneman, *Thinking, Fast and Slow* (Farrar, Straus, and Giroux, 2011), www. fsgbooks.com.

HEARING FROM GOD?

It is interesting that the four-hundred-year period before the Advent of the Christ is referred to as a time of silence. Some biblical scholars have intimated that God was not speaking, but perhaps what they really mean is there was no recorded speech from God that survived.

Clearly, Simeon and Anna had heard from God. I suspect the Lord of the universe has never been silent, except to those who choose not to hear him or do not know him.

But if you believe the Holy Spirit does speak to you, can I advise a little caution?

Biblical illiteracy is widespread in the American church and worldwide. We believers who have the entirety of the inspired Word generally have no excuse for not being familiar with it, yet most believers I meet and work with know very little, except what they hear from the pulpit or a podcast.

If you are not spending substantial time dwelling in the Word, be very careful with what you think you hear from a spirit. The Holy Spirit is not the only spiritual being out there; Satan and his demons are active in the world as well. Further, we are all capable of having our own thoughts and easily pronouncing them to be from the Spirit. We promote ourselves to a godlike status when we uncritically accept every thought in our head as inspired.

Here is the critical test, delivered through an ancient prophet named Malachi: "For I the Lord do not change."

The Holy Spirit will never give you a word that contradicts who God has already revealed himself to be. God will not tell you to violate the standards of truth and righteousness he has already made clear.

This is why you need to know the whole Bible. It is the revelation of God.

This means more than just it being revealed by him, for the entirety of it reveals his beautiful heart. The Bible in its entirety reveals who he is. You can only fully experience God and hear from him properly if you know how to recognize a spirit as counterfeit (or your own spirit of selfishness), if what you are hearing is not in line with who God already revealed himself to be.

> **TAKEAWAY 3:** If you consider yourself Spirit-led but do not have a full knowledge of the whole Bible, get into the Word. Be very careful about believing any voices you hear until you have a more complete revelation of who God is through extensive reading and reflection.

Chapter Two

A SEVERE BLESSING

Mary, Mother of Jesus

THIS DOESN'T SEEM REAL.

But he told me this day would come.

I stood there with John and the other women, watching my son die. He didn't even look human; his face was caked in blood, contorted; he was writhing in pain.

I knew the traditions of my people. I was supposed to be wailing and dramatic.

But he had told me this day would come. And I had been warned long before that; it had been the old man Simeon who said, "A sword will pierce your very soul,"[16] when Yeshua was just a baby. I didn't really understand. Now I stood silently, still not really able to understand. Today, I was feeling the sword.

His eyes suddenly met mine; he nodded his head slightly. "It's okay, Mama; it'll all be okay."

That boy. He had done that since he was a child; his voice was in my head as clearly as if he had said the words out loud.

---

16 Luke 2:35 NLT.

It had been a strange journey with this one.

But it was wonderful too.

I remember when my father told me I was to be married. I can't say I was thrilled, but being a poor girl from Nazareth, it wasn't necessarily a bad deal. But I was so young, I was scared of being a wife. Joseph was a bit older than me, but he seemed to be a very gentle and sweet man. He loved his mom and his sisters, and he treated me with such respect and kindness. He probably was the sweetest man in Nazareth.

But still, there was that whole knowing one another thing, living with a man I hardly knew, and most likely, there were going to be children—soon. I still felt like a child myself, and I kind of wanted to stay that way. I had seen children being born and didn't really want anything to do with that.

After Joseph asked my father if he could marry me and we were betrothed, he kept asking, "Are you okay with this?"

I guess he could sense I really wasn't.

I wanted to say no.

But for some reason, I sensed the Lord was leading me into this. Why? I did not know. I fully believed I would be a horrid wife and mother. I was just a girl.

"Yes," I heard myself tell my husband-to-be, "I think it is what the Lord wants us to do." I was saying what sounded right, but I wasn't really sure even I believed it. I wasn't sure Joseph believed me, either.

Poor man; was I the best he could do?

It all seemed so silly; I was a nobody. Why would the Lord talk to someone like me? There were other young girls in Nazareth; we played together and shared our dreams of being married to great men and having lots of children around us. We dreamed of walking through town with our husbands and seeing everyone smile as we led a train of children behind us.

I wasn't the prettiest or smartest; I was just Mary from Nazareth, daughter of Michael. I would be married and become a mother, just like every other Jewish girl. I guessed it would be fine. It was probably the best future I could hope for.

I looked at my boy again. It seemed like he was gone, but then he pulled himself up and screamed.

Chills went down my back. My tears were flowing, but I still wasn't able to make a sound. I wept in silence.

This was the way of dying on a cross. It wasn't the first time I had seen this.

I wish I had never seen it.

The Romans kept us all fearful through things like crucifixion. Or they would take all of our money as taxes—or sometimes a family member, if someone had no money. At other times, they passed out bread. You never knew where you stood with the Romans; they just made it clear they wouldn't accept insubordination.

I didn't like their manipulation. My Yeshua had taught me a lot about fear and about courage. The Romans used fear as their primary weapon. My boy taught me to be courageous.

I needed that. I wasn't always courageous. I wasn't really anybody. I had felt worthless for most of my life.

I remembered that morning well, one of the most fearful days of my life.

My parents had left the house early to do some business in town. I had a rare moment in the house alone, or so I thought.

I went up on the roof just to breathe for a minute. The weight of my upcoming marriage was heavy on my heart. But it was a beautiful cool morning. I thought it would be relaxing to sit on the roof for a while and just watch the world waking up. I loved it up on the roof by myself. I could dream of a better life, enjoy the birds, watch people, and just be calm.

I sat down, closed my eyes, and took a deep breath. I smelled the flowers, listened to the birds, and could even hear a few people talking in the houses near ours. Suddenly, I felt a very cool breeze; it was as though a large bird had flown right past me. I opened my eyes to see it, and I screamed.

There was a man, or something like a man, standing right in front of me on the roof. I hadn't heard the old wooden ladder creaking. He was just suddenly there, tall, muscular, and just a bit strange in his appearance; he was a man, but it was as if there was a power or light coming from him. I was frozen in fear. I wanted to run, but I could not move. I had looked down instinctively, but then I heard the kindest and most unusual voice I had ever heard from a man (or whatever this was).

"Greetings, favored woman. The Lord is with you."

I was cross-legged on the roof, with my nose nearly touching the floor. I was breathing hard, my heart was racing furiously, and I felt I was going to pass out.

What did he say, "favored woman"? I thought to myself, *He must think I'm someone else.*

And then he laughed, a beautiful and full-bellied laugh.

I slowly raised my head and looked at his face.

He was laughing at me, but not in an unkind way. It seemed clear he had heard my thoughts.

I was now searching this man's face. He was looking at me as if he was seeing some great treasure. He appeared thrilled, in awe, so much so I looked back to see if someone else was behind me.

He laughed again, and our eyes met. He was thoroughly enjoying this rooftop meeting.

I was not.

"The Lord is with you"? That is what he had said. Why? How? Why me? I was a nobody, plain ol' Mary from Nazareth. Favored woman? Am I even a woman yet?

I mused to myself, *I don't think I want to be a woman.*

Even more laughter poured out from the tall man; this was too much. He was hearing my thoughts. He was enjoying me way too much. I felt faint again, and then—

"Do not be afraid, Mary, for you have found favor with God."[17]

He knew my name? This message from this person was for me?

"You who would destroy the temple and rebuild it in three days, save yourself!"[18]

I was brought back to the moment by the shouts at my boy. It was three Pharisees, taunting my perfect son, laughing and shaking their heads at my boy. I locked eyes with these religious men; I don't know what they saw, but I felt sorry for them. If only they only knew Yeshua like I did, even partly as well as I did, they would worship him if they did.

How was it that these men who spent so much time in the scrolls couldn't see who he was? Why are men so easily deceived and distracted from what is right in front of their noses? How many miracles and prophecies had been fulfilled right in front of them, and all the while they taunted and harassed my boy?

---

[17] Luke 1:30 NLT.
[18] Matthew 27:40 ESV.

But then, oh my, did I ever struggle with figuring out who Yeshua was. Oh sure, I knew how I got pregnant. But once I held him in my arms, he just seemed like every other baby, small child, and growing boy I had ever known. He had to learn things, just like I did when I was young. He had to figure out who he was. That was odd, for God.

I remember him coming back from the synagogue, having spent the day reading the scrolls. He would recite Isaiah to me and excitedly say, "I think it is speaking of me, Mama." I would smile, agreeing outwardly, but inwardly, I was terrified. What would everyone think of a boy who considered himself to be the Messiah? Especially being the son of Joseph and Mary; sure, we were in the lineage of David and Judah, but we weren't very high in the social structure, even in Nazareth. Surely, he would come through someone more well-known, more respectable, more wealthy?

When Yeshua began teaching, what all of us really struggled with was his lack of law-giving. His most common teaching was just "follow me." A lot of people tried to; it was confusing and hard.

He shared a lot of admonishments and principles; it was all powerful. But most of it focused on just the two big laws he so often stressed: love God with all you have, and love your neighbor as you love yourself.

It was a lot easier to pick and choose some commands from the law and try to keep them, but following Yeshua caused pain. He was free of prejudice, had no resentment, and was so courageous to go anywhere people needed him. When I tried to go along with him, the beauty of who he was exposed the ugliness inside of me. Me, his mother?

That was the pain. I saw him love people who tried to kill him, while I still hated the people who had excluded me when they thought I was an adulteress.

It was so humbling. How could my child be so much more loving and patient than me?

I was his mother? It just didn't seem possible.

I told him once I was the wrong person to be his mother. He looked at me seriously and asked, "So, the Lord made a mistake when he gave us each other?"

"No, no, no, I am not criticizing the Lord. Oh, my, yes, I am. I am so s-s-sorry," I stammered through tears.

He hugged me. "You have such a hard job being my mother. But you were the right girl for the job."

Those words about it being hard to be his parents; he had spoken of that from his early days, as he began to figure out who he was. We thought it was some sort of false humility at times, and Joseph and I had gotten on him once because we thought he was wanting our praise. He took it well; he always was a dream child in that respect. He was so patient with us.

It was only later that we understood he realized being parents of the Messiah was an impossible assignment. It was something one could only do through the power of the Spirit of God. And that made it beautiful and special. It was beyond hard; we just had to get up each day and keep moving, one step at a time, in faith.

"He still loves you, you know?" I heard myself say weakly to the three Pharisees.

They looked surprised, recognizing me as the mother of the one on the cross. They each looked down and then walked away. My words sounded kind. My boy had taught me much, but I still was struggling in my heart not to strangle each of them. Part of me wanted to hurt them, badly.

Part of me deeply desired to kill each one, slowly.

But then he, my beautiful son, now seemed to live inside of me.

I suddenly realized it had become very dark, though it was the middle of the day.

Darkness.

I went back to that day on the roof with the angel; this imposing laughing creature knew my name. The Lord knew my name? I couldn't seem to wrap my heart around this; Nazareth wasn't very big, but it seemed very few people knew my name (or even seemed to care to). I suddenly remembered the story we heard in the synagogue about Father Abraham when he had a child by the woman Hagar. When she ran away, the Lord found her and called her back; she told the Lord, "You are a God of seeing."[19]

And the angel who found her knew her name.

This was real.

This was the God of the stories I had heard all my life. He knows my name? He sees me? I was suddenly thrilled. I wanted to sing to my Lord.

"Behold, you will conceive in your womb and bear a son, and you shall call his name Jesus. He will be great and will be called the Son of the Most High. And the Lord God will give to him the throne of his father David, and he will reign over the house of Jacob forever, and of his kingdom there will be no end."[20]

What?

How could this be?

---

[19] Genesis 16:13 ESV.

[20] Luke 1:31–33 ESV.

This can't be real.

My heart was racing again, and I was once again face down on the roof. I don't understand; this can't be. He has the wrong girl; my life is set, I am marrying Joseph, and I will have his children. Maybe that's it. I gathered my courage; I was shaking, but he had to mean this was going to be Joseph's child, right?

I struggled to find the words.

"How will this be, since I am a virgin?" My voice was cracking from the strain, my tears were flowing, and my eyes were tightly closed. Please, Lord, I don't understand. Let this be Joseph's child. Please let it be Joseph's child. This was so confusing; had I not been dreading that whole knowing Joseph as his wife? Now I was begging to have his child? I was so much the wrong girl for this.

I felt a gentle but strong hand on my chin, and my face was pulled upward. I peeked out of one eye; the angel smiled gently, laughed a little, and then held my face in both of his hands.

He said slowly, "The Holy Spirit will come upon you, and the power of the Most High will overshadow you; therefore the child to be born will be called—"

His voice was suddenly confused in my head; I felt a great darkness come over me. This was not going to be Joseph's child? What does he mean, "the Holy Spirit will come upon you"? What does that even look like? Joseph will leave me; I know he will. My abba, he will not believe me. How do I answer him? He will ask, "Who did this to you?"

I cannot say, "The Holy Spirit came upon me." That? No, he will not accept that blasphemy.

My face was very hot, and I felt like the house was collapsing beneath me. I opened my eyes once again, and the angel was still looking intently at me.

He said, "Your relative Elizabeth in her old age has also conceived a son, and this is the sixth month with her who was called barren. For nothing is impossible with God."[21]

Elizabeth, with child? For some reason, this calmed me, or maybe it was the solid hand of the angel on my face. Elizabeth had always loved me and treated me like I was her own daughter. Maybe it was because she had longed for children of her own? She was expecting? That would be wonderful. She was way past the age of being pregnant. Maybe we could do this together. I was so terrified.

I looked back at the angel; he was looking at me, patient, yet with a raised eyebrow. Angels have eyebrows? Wait until I tell my girlfriends that. I smiled a bit at the thought. The angel smiled back but continued to wait.

I suddenly realized I was being given a choice.

A choice was mine to make. I rarely was allowed to choose anything, but this?

I didn't see any way, couldn't imagine me being ... everyone would reject me, right? Joseph was a good man; he would not believe this. He would not take me as his wife; he deserved a good girl. I might be stoned to death; my family will disown me. Who am I to raise the Lord's child? I am just a girl. I can't be a mother, not this mother.

I pulled my head away and turned to the side. I was staring at the roof. I could say no. The angel was giving me a choice; the Lord was giving me a choice.

---

[21] Luke 1:36–37 ESV.

Being Joseph's wife wouldn't be so bad; other friends had married in a similar way.

I don't understand how to do what I am being asked to do; I'm not brave. I'm not smart. I can't do this alone. But I will be alone; no one will believe me.

My mind was a jumbled mess. I cannot understand what I am being told; this overshadowing by the Most High—what would that be like? It sounded terrifying.

The most obvious answer is no. I cannot see any way of doing what I am being asked to do.

You are a God of seeing.

The Lord knows my name, though; he sent this angel here to me on the roof on a day when I was alone. He isn't forcing me to do this. He treasures me? He sees me? Why?

I slowly turned back to the angel and looked upward; his head was turned slightly, inquisitive still. I was breathing hard; my heart was racing. I suddenly couldn't swallow. I felt like I was suffocating.

"I … I am the Lord's servant," I said. "May everything you have said about me come true."[22]

The angel burst out laughing, with tears rolling down his cheek, then he hugged me tightly, so tightly that I closed my eyes again. There was a sudden cool wind; I opened my eyes, and he was gone.

Angels hug, angels cry; wait until my girlfriends hear that.

I collapsed and curled up into a ball and cried. My heart felt like it would burst, and my breathing was fast. I closed my eyes tightly and lay there for a long time.

I was brought back to the moment by the sound of crying.

I looked at Mary Magdalene, who stood beside me, weeping.

---

[22] Luke 1:38 NLT.

She had spoken to me once of what her life had been like before my son cast the demons from her. She kept saying how dark it had been, how horrible and terrified she was every day because she never knew what the demons would compel her to do to the people she loved. She spoke much of my boy bringing her light and being her light.

These people were killing the light today. As dark as this day was, I feared for my people for the days to come. My son had prophesied of a time when horrible things would take place, and those of us in Judea were to "flee to the mountains"[23] to find safety. He had explained to me the beautiful but very just nature of the Father in heaven; murdering the Son would not go unpunished. As dark as this day was, there was a horrible day coming soon for Judea.

I remembered some other terrible days, but I had to escape this darkness for a moment, so I thought back and remembered a special moment, one that Yeshua used to tell others about with great delight.

I was helping with a friend's wedding in Cana. I had been there a couple of days to get things ready, but my Yeshua arrived later. We had more guests than planned, and the wine was running low.

I ran to him and said, "They have no wine."[24]

I had never seen him roll his eyes before, but this time he did. "Woman, what does this have to do with me? My hour has not yet come."[25]

There were times when I just did not accept *no* from my

[23] Matthew 24:16 ESV.
[24] John 2:3 ESV.
[25] John 2:4 ESV.

children. This boy, from even before I carried him, had caused me so much grief. When Jesus would tell the story later to his disciples, this is what tickled him most.

In spite of his pronouncement about his "time" and me knowing who he was, I just went ahead and told the servants at the wedding feast, "Do whatever he tells you." And then I walked away.

Oh, it's so embarrassing to think about now, now that my faith in him is so strong. But I was just a mom; I knew at least some of what he was capable of. "Do whatever he tells you"? I suppose he could have told them nothing, but he was always the best son.

"Well, sure, I'm the Messiah, but she is my mother." My son told this mom story anywhere to those who were closest to him. It used to be embarrassing, but then, it was just the confusion that went along with being the mother of God.

Yes, he made wine; he made great wine. It was effortless; it smelled great, tasted great, and he did it with nearly no witnesses or fanfare. But the whispered words of the miracle began spreading within minutes.

Of course, there was a story behind my insistence on him fixing the wine problem; on occasion as he grew, little Yeshua made things happen. He was always very discreet, and at first, Joseph and I kind of just overlooked it. I suppose it was so hard to comprehend that we chose just to turn away. But there was finally a day when we couldn't. I had several children at the time, and Joseph was working hard to support us all. Yeshua could tell I was very tired and frazzled, and one day, I walked into the house after nursing one of my babies to find a very nice meal prepared. I was so thrilled, but then something struck me; I had been sitting just outside in the shade of the roof for only a few minutes. How had he done this?

There was food, nearly all of it, that we didn't have in the house. The oven was unlit, no coals, and there was no mess.

"Son, where did you get this food?" I asked.

"I made it for you, Mama; let's eat," was his answer, motioning for me to sit on the floor as he took the baby from me.

"Answer me, where did you get this? You haven't built a fire the oven. You didn't leave the house." I was insistent.

"Oh, Mom, you worry too much. I made this for you; let us eat before it gets cold."

He sat down and looked back at me, with that cute little dimpled smirk he had shown since he was a baby.

"Sit down, Mama, it's okay," I heard him say, though no one else heard a thing.

That boy. I know most moms say they know when something is wrong with one of their children, even when they can't see them, but this boy could speak to me without opening his mouth. I wondered if he would still speak to me when he was gone.

I hoped and prayed he would.

It was still dark.

John was suddenly beside me. He was a very sensitive yet strong man, not unlike my boy Yeshua. They were best friends. John was always coming into my home and telling me great stories of what my boy had done that day. It seemed he loved my special boy as much as I did. We both stared at the man on the cross, the God on the cross.

Yeshua looked at us.

"Woman, behold your son."[26]

I looked at John. He smiled when he heard that, while tears still

---

[26] John 19:26.

flowed freely down his face and into his beard. He was younger than my boy, but he was looking haggard and much older now. This was as hard on him as it was on me. No one loved Yeshua as much as John and I did.

"Behold, your mother."[27]

It was a brief moment of joy during a dreadful day. And it was so typical of my son. He was a King, the Messiah, and Immanuel. And yet, his heart was always outward toward others. Even in the midst of his great suffering, he was concerned for John and the woman, the special name he used for me sometime because of our long talks about it seeming wrong for me to be the mother of God himself. I still felt like a girl. He called me woman.

His woman was treasured and valued; he truly admired me and always wanted the best for me. He always looked at me like I was someone very special and precious. From the moment with the angel on the roof, those from heaven saw me as a jewel. He was the Son of seeing, even what I had trouble seeing in myself.

The best, that was what he wanted for everyone, and would give to anyone who accepted that wild invitation: "follow me."

"It is finished!"

His voice was loud, determined, and victorious. We stood there for a long time, feeling pain and emptiness, and what a beautiful and incomprehensible sight it was. It happened just like he told us it would.

"We should go home, Mother," John said, taking my hand in his.

I looked at John; he, too, was a treasure. I knew he could see it in my eyes.

"Yes, son, take me home."

---

[27] John 19:27.

UNPACKING MARY'S SEVERE BLESSING

We who believe in the Way naturally revere heroic Bible characters such as Mary.

Yet Mary, in what little the scripture records of her words and thoughts, struggled greatly with one of the most challenging and overwhelming missions ever recorded.

As a very young woman, she was asked to experience becoming pregnant in a way never heard of, to bear someone who already existed, and to be mother to Immanuel—God with us.

It was an impossible assignment to understand, much less carry out.

I perceive the Lord of all has a mission for each of us today; it intimidates and overwhelms us, even though it is likely nowhere near the scary incomprehensibility of mothering God himself.

So what can we learn from Mary about saying okay to what God asks us to do?

ONE STEP AT A TIME

Contrary to common Christian folk wisdom, God often asks us to join him in doing things that will be very hard, distressing, and possibly fatal.

As it was brought out in this enhanced story, the words of the angel may not have made a lot of sense to Mary. It was confusing (the Spirit will come upon you?) and potentially dangerous and life-threatening (when your father asks who got you pregnant, how will he receive "The Spirit of God got me pregnant?" Sounds blasphemous.), and represented something completely out of the realm of human experience to that point, ever.

So in reference to the often-repeated Christian folk wisdom ("If it is God's will, you will have a sense of peace about it"), maybe not so much? Shortly after receiving the angelic visit and news of her Messiah-bearing pregnancy, Mary goes to see Elizabeth (her relative and soon-to-be mother of John the Baptist); was she escaping a bit? How much did her father and mother know, and when? Did they believe her?

The big point here: Mary teaches us that walking and working where the Lord ask us to go may put us in a position of crisis, fear, and feeling completely overwhelmed.

If we feel unable to do what our Father puts before us, we are correct. He did not give Mary an assignment she could look at and say, "I got this." I suspect there were many sleepless nights and tear-filled prayers, asking her Maker for a whole bunch of faith and help.

This is a consistent theme of people in the Bible chosen by God to do his work. Just read what is commonly called "Faith's Hall of Fame" found in Hebrews 11. In this chapter are some of the great heroes of the faith, who were nothing more than ordinary people like us who heard God's call and just said, "Well, okay, I trust you."

TAKEAWAY 1: Don't look for a sense of peace if God is calling you to join him in his work. Instead, know him well enough through his Word to be sure what you are doing is in line with who he is, and then walk one step at a time as he works through you.

MARY'S GROWTH INVOLVED
INTENSE SUFFERING

While being the mother of the promised Messiah was in a way thrilling and doubtless had many joys, from the early days, she was warned of the coming pain.

Remember the story from the first chapter on Simeon and his prophetic words that a sword would pierce her heart?

She would always remember the angelic visit, the way in which she became pregnant, and the prophetic words of people such as Simeon and Anna, but still in so many ways, Jesus was just like any other baby and growing child.

Even on her best day with Jesus, the promised sword hovered near her heart. When would the other shoe drop?

If you are seeking God with all your heart and perceive his call to work for his kingdom, do not expect anything less than what Mary experienced. Expect uncertainty, opposition, and dark nights of the soul, pouring your tears and your heart out to God.

> **TAKEAWAY 2:** Do not expect the assignments God puts in your life to be easy. We grow through challenge, suffering, and struggle. Embrace it; go all in, like Mary (you can't be just sort of pregnant with the Messiah).

STAND FIRM AND BE HONEST WITH GOD
AND OTHERS IN YOUR UNCERTAINTY

Mary struggled with who Jesus was throughout her life. If you struggle with our Lord in your life, you are in good company.

It is clear from reading Luke's Gospel letter that he interviewed Mary. In two places, he records that Mary pondered or treasured events with Jesus in her heart.[28]

In spite of the visit and words from the angel, in spite of knowing how she got pregnant, she still struggled to figure out her little boy, who was to be her Savior.

In view of that, should we expect that we will ever have Yeshua of Nazareth, fully God and fully man, completely figured out?

In your walk with Jesus, if you are sometimes unsure of what to do, who he is, or even if he is really there, welcome to being his disciple. None of his closest disciples who walked with him really got him, hence, they all abandoned him in the garden before his trial. This in spite of the fact that he told them he was going to die and they would abandon him.

So if you feel ashamed of your "three-steps-forward, two-steps-back" walk with Jesus, just think about one of the prophecies about him: "He will not cry aloud or lift up his voice, or make it heard in the street; a bruised reed he will not break, and a faintly burning wick he will not quench."[29]

To put it plainly, Jesus did not come in his full glory and overwhelm us with fear. Instead, he came humbly and quietly, as a human baby. He approaches us gently, and when he sees someone with a delicate and sometimes uncertain faith (the "bruised reed" or "faintly burning wick"), he does not despise or quench it; he gets us. He lived in a body like us in the world we live in. He knows our fears, our weaknesses, and our limitations.

If you feel your faith is uncertain and Yeshua the Messiah is

---

[28] See Luke 2:19, 2:51.
[29] Isaiah 42:2, 3.

disappointed that you are not some unstoppable warrior of faith at all times, just think of his sweet mother.

She struggled to comprehend who her precious miracle boy was all the days of his life—and likely beyond.

And that was the way of the woman who changed the Savior's diaper and fed him from her own breast.

TAKEAWAY 3: The way of walking with the Messiah we know as Jesus is full of uncertainty and is at times hard to comprehend. Be like Mary; hold fast to what you know, and be honest with the Lord, who loves you in your times of weakness and doubt.

Chapter Three

LIKE THE WIND?

Nicodemus, the Pharisees, and the Holy Spirit

"You?"

"Yes, Pilate," I replied, "may I go prepare the body—"

"But you? You're one of them," he interrupted, looking at my ornamented robe.

"I know, I know; can I please see his body?" I pleaded.

"But it was your people who demanded that he die," he objected.

I grabbed my robe at the collar, ripped it strongly, and shouted, "I am of Christ."

Pilate's mouth dropped open; his attendants looked shocked and scared. He stared at me briefly and then looked down at his feet.

I calmed myself, lowered my voice. Apologetically, I said, "Please, may I prepare his body?"

He interrupted again, still looking down. His voice was quiet and unsteady.

"The darkness," he said, and his voice was trembling.

"Yes, umm, that was, ah—" My voice trailed off, thinking it

was like nothing I had ever lived through in my many years. But it matched the mood of my heart. The regrets began again; I had been face-to-face with him. "He did say that he was light."

"People have flooded my chambers with reports of the dead walking the streets, proclaiming that he was—" He was still looking down, his body was shaking. Pilate was crying.

So was I. So was I.

"Sir, I plead with you, may I go to him?" I needed to see him, to do one good thing to him for showing me, for showing me ... what?

"My wife, she warned me not to hurt him," he said quietly, now looking straight at me. His eyes were puffy and red; tears streamed down his face—this usually fearsome-looking man suddenly appeared as a small and very frightened boy.

He looked down again. "What does this all mean, Nicodemus?"

I looked at him, hunched over, looking as weak as I felt. Did I feel sorry for him? I felt sorry for Pilate?

This Yeshua had changed everything. What I said, it wasn't my typical delivery style of my old days of pride as a leader of my people. I hardly recognized my own voice.

"Well, sir, he was, umm, he is God, himself. And we, uh—"

"What will become of me? I knew I shouldn't, but the people wanted him."

Pilate slowly stood and turned away, head bowed, and walked toward the door.

"Take him to the—" He paused; I thought he was going to say "man." But the word he spoke, it sucked the air out of the room.

"King."

He spoke the word quietly, reverently.

One of Pilate's attendants, trembling, came to me and gently took my arm. "I'll show you—" He stopped in mid-sentence. There was an air of grief so thick in the palace; it was the saddest place I had ever been.

We walked through rooms and halls to a darkened room lit by candles.

Joseph[30] was already there. He was wealthy, like me, but he had figured out Yeshua much quicker than I. He looked up when I walked in, a blood-soaked fragment of clothing in his hands, and nodded.

"I had a feeling you'd be here; he spoke of you often."

He spoke of me? What had he said? I couldn't quite seem to go all in with him, like so many did. For all my years of study of the Torah, the writings, for all my effort, his teaching, well, the rabbi from Nazareth threw me for a loop.

I remember the first time I had seen him. We in the council were getting more frequent reports of a rabbi who spoke like no other and who was healing people.

Strange, but amongst those of us on the council, the reaction was nearly immediate. This man had to be a fraud. Once we had gotten just a little whiff of his teachings, plus, I suppose the fact that he had not been the disciple of any of us, as far as we knew, we decided he had to a heretic, like the others.

Of course, there was the fact that many of the common people, having been to the rabbi, were asking us whether or not he was the Messiah. Given the fact that false Messiahs had been popping up for decades, this had predisposed us to deny that anyone could be him; it was understandable. But now, looking back, it might have

---

[30] Joseph of Arimathea, found in Matthew 27:57–61.

been better if we had slowed down a bit and considered what this man was actually teaching.

So that first time, I had volunteered to go and investigate the new teacher, along with Shabtai of Bethany. He was young and on fire for law-keeping, just as I once was.

Just as I once was.

For so much of my life, I was so sure I could keep the laws and be right with God. I spent so much time studying, praying, and attempting to fortify my resolve to stop sinning. I think I really believed I could brace myself morally and do it all right; I guess a lot of us believe we are better than we are. I had been quite good at making life line up properly and doing what was expected of me earlier in life, but the older I got, the tougher it was.

Shabtai and I arrived at the place where the Nazarene was. He was putting his hands on people, healing them, laughing, and hugging. We stood at a distance, arms crossed, determined to find out what heresies he was guilty of.

Something really bothered us after a few minutes; I suppose it was the contrast between those of us who were religious experts and himself when we were around people.

We Pharisees, the priests, and even the scribes were so stuffy, so somber-looking, we demanded respect.

This Yeshua, he blended in with everyone; we would not have noticed him had it not been for the crowds that flocked to him. He seemed truly unconcerned with what anyone thought of him or that we Pharisees in our impressive robes were watching him; he was just who he was. But there was something remarkable, that contrast between him and us; his face was kind, full of joy, and, well, oozing with love for everyone he met.

His laughter was unrestrained. When he healed someone, they would sometimes cry with happiness, and he would laugh this beautiful laugh; it was like a parent watching a child open a special gift. He found true joy in the joy of others.

That bothered me.

At first, we suspected the people he seemed to be healing were a setup. That is, we believed they were working for him, pretending to be ill, and then they would suddenly claim to be better once he had touched them. I went to a few of them just to confirm this to be true; they all seemed genuinely confused by my questions. "What do you mean, was our son really blind?"

Some even accused me of being blind, and now I see they were right. It just took me a while to see my blindness, but the embers of discomfort about this man began on that first day when I heard him speak.

"You have heard that it was said, 'You shall not commit adultery.'"[31]

That got my attention.

What was he going to dispute about that? He had been, pretty solidly, I must admit, taking down some teachings we Pharisees had specialized in, but adultery? That was a no-brainer, right?

"But I say to you that everyone who looks at a woman with lustful intent has already committed adultery with her in his heart,"[32] he said. I could have sworn as he said it that he made direct eye contact with me.

I suddenly felt a flush of heat and anger—no, seething rage

---

[31] Matthew 5:27.
[32] Matthew 5:28.

began welling up inside of my heart. How dare he lecture me, but was he?

It suddenly struck me; why did this above all things affect me in such a way? My heart thought back to … but I was fearful to go there. There had been, many years ago, that woman. She was beautiful, and I was a young rabbi, beginning to get quite a following.

She was eager for the words and so affirming, attentive, and, perhaps, vulnerable. Nothing really happened between us, but in my heart, oh, did things ever happen. In my heart, she and I had an ongoing, passionate relationship; we did things that even after all these years, the thoughts of my heart condemned me.

But we hadn't—well, it's not like I ever, but I had eventually gone too far. I found myself thinking about her, scheming to find her in town, and bringing up special teachings for her after my normal times of speaking.

We grew close, and then there was that day when she came to the temple and sought me out because of a hurt done to her. We embraced, my hands went—well, it still hurts to think about it.

She ran from the temple, crying. I had betrayed a trust by beginning to do those things I first created in my mind. Yes, "lustful intent" was the issue. She had come to the very temple of God, only to be accosted by a rabbi.

I lived for years in fear of being found out, but my victim remained silent. No one saw us, technically nothing happened that could be proved under the law.

He was right; just not technically joining with someone did not make one holy. I looked up at the rabbi again. His kind eyes were locked on me. I looked down, and for the first time since that day twenty years ago, tears of grief and shame flowed for what I had done to that precious daughter of God. I had been married when it happened; I'm pretty sure my wife suspected.

I turned away to leave; I heard Shabtai ask me, "Nicodemus, where are you—?"

I waved my hand and muttered, "I must go; you stay and listen."

And then I heard the true rabbi, still teaching, say, "No one can."[33]

I stopped and turned my head, straining to hear what no one could do, according to this teacher, who had just sunk a spiritual dagger into my deceptive old heart.

"No one can serve two masters, for either he will hate the one and love the other, or he will be devoted to one and despise the other."[34]

I stood there for a moment and then turned fully toward the Nazarene and slowly looked up at him. He was, again, staring straight at me.

Two masters?

Was he suggesting that I was serving two masters?

I turned and began walking quickly back to the temple. My thoughts were racing. I was serving the Lord, right? That is why I spent so much time studying the commands. That is why I tried so hard to show people my holiness, to be an example, to show the way to God.

Or was I? Was I trying to make much of the Lord, or was I—

I was walking past a stream bed, and there were some small trees; I went and sat on the ground in the shade, lost in thought.

---

[33] Matthew 6:24.

[34] Ibid.

Why did the rabbi from Nazareth radiate such joy, such a love for life and people? He seemed unconcerned with himself, unlike me. I thought through everything I said or did. Was it for God?

Was everything I had done actually for God?

This sudden conviction, revealed through a flood of memories of the woman, my dishonesty with my wife, my fear of the disapproval of the high priest and council. I was doing what I was doing, in trying to make me appear to be … respectable? Holy?

My master was not the Lord? It was me?

I was glorifying me; I was fearful of the disapproval of man. Oh sure, I would teach that adultery was wrong, but as the teacher had said, in my heart, unspeakable things had happened between me and the woman in the temple, in the temple, of all places. I had devoted my life to establishing myself as a man of holiness, respectability, pride, leadership, and faith?

I was hiding, just as pathetically as Adam in the garden, trying to cover his shame with a fig leaf.

Two masters. I loved me and hated God.

Was that the source of my somber face? Was that why I rarely laughed, why my face looked like a joyless and frozen mask most of the time? Because I was afraid of being found out for who I was? I was hiding who I really was.

I pulled off a strip of cloth from his body, dried and stuck to the raw muscle underneath. I grabbed a piece of linen, dipped it in the hyssop water Joseph had brought, and gently, as though he were still alive, cleaned him as best I could.

I was returning a blessing, in such a small and meaningless way. I was too late.

His teachings had been the painful beginning of a healing. He uncovered wounds I did not know I had.

I remembered watching him talk, heal, and just live among the people; there was something beautiful, even stunning in the way he treated people. Yes, I started following him, from a safe distance.

This man was anything but safe, at least for a fearful self-worshipper like me.

The way he went to people, the worst of people, it undid me.

It didn't matter how evil or dirty I thought they were, love just emanated from him. I was intrigued.

I took a chance; I went to him one night, hoping no one would see me. It would endanger my position on the council to be seen with the Nazarene.

However, it was clear to me and some of my fellow Pharisees that this man had to be from God. The stories of the miracles, including some we had seen with our own eyes, were mounting. We quietly assembled in a small, safe group. Could this teacher be the promised suffering servant, the Messiah, that the prophet Isaiah had foretold?[35]

I remember working through one of his followers, arranging the meeting, and changing into some borrowed clothes, trying not to be recognized. I knew how to hide who I was so well, only this time, I was hiding from my own kind. I went to the house as instructed, one dark night.

I sat down with him, a small lamp on the table illuminated his kind face. I was nervous, as nervous as I have ever been. My mouth was dry; my heart was beating fast. I wasn't thinking or speaking clearly. This man, he must be from God. Maybe he was God? I had

---

[35] See Isaiah 50 and following chapters.

spent my life trying to be godly, to please God, to find the secret to perfect obedience and holiness, yet of late, as I looked at myself and my fellow strivers, I had this nagging question.

Can this negative, bitter, proud, and critical way of life be from God? Is this why God spoke through the prophets? Was the way we did worship and life really what our Maker intended?

I still tried to teach the party line to the synagogue, but I was full of doubt, and I was becoming cynical. I suspected some of our group were picking up on my tone.

So on that night, face-to-face with the miracle worker from God, I tried to ask what I most wanted to know: "Rabbi, we know that you are teacher come from God, for no one can do these signs that you do unless God is with him."[36]

Funny, it wasn't really a question per se, but he understood what I was asking.

What he said threw me off, big time: "Truly, truly, I say to you, unless one is born again he cannot see the kingdom of God."[37]

Honestly, I thought he was out of his mind. Born again? It made no sense. I was a very mature follower of God; I really just wanted that final step of wisdom to help me to grow to see, to feel, to be a mature and joyous lover of God, like he was. I had spent years, no, decades, immersed in the Holy Word; surely, all I needed was just a small tweak in my spirituality, just one more expounding of spiritual principle to become, well, what he seemed to be.

"How can a man be born when he is old?"[38] I really could not understand what he was asking me to do.

---

[36] John 3:2.

[37] Ibid., v. 3.

[38] Ibid., v. 4.

Tonight, when I ripped my robe—the robe I had worked so hard to earn, the robe that told the people around me of my importance, my high status, and represented my glory—when I tore it, I began the path to being born again.

In that moment of ripping my robe, I realized I had always relied on myself and my performance for safety and significance. I covered the tracks of my sin with little keepings of the law, and that impressed many. But in my heart, I was full of fear, shame, and anger.

In the eyes of the Nazarene, he saw right through me.

In front of Pilate, I suddenly threw myself around the arms of the Messiah. I suddenly didn't care if I lived or died. I didn't care what Pilate or any of my council members thought. I just trusted that this dead man in front of me was not a mere man, nor was he truly dead.

He was who he said he was; he was the eternal King. I reached down and began opening the spices and cleansing agents I had brought with me. Joseph watched me begin the process of preparing his shredded body for burial.

"Do you need some help?" he asked gently.

"Yes, Joseph, I need a lot of help, thank you," and a small laugh of joy escaped my mouth. I had long been the man people went to in order to get help in being right with God. This was the first time in a long time I had admitted to anyone I needed help.

I needed more help than any man or woman could give me.

There was the one other thing Jesus had said that first time we talked that I was beginning to grasp.

In my unspoken question, he knew what I needed to hear.

And he knew I couldn't handle it, at least not on that dark night sitting face-to-face with the Messiah: "Do not marvel that I said to you, 'You must be born again.' The wind blows where it wishes and you hear its sound, but you do not know where it comes from or where it goes. So it is with everyone who is born of the Spirit."[39]

I had spent my whole life keeping the rules. I thought I was good at it. I may have fooled others about my holiness; I think I even fooled myself, but this perfect God-man, the Messiah, saw the ugliness in me and called me on it.

It was the beginning of the ultimate healing.

I had been a fool, blind to what the law should have showed me from the beginning.

The whole time, the law was designed to teach me I could not do life with God without his power. It never occurred to me until now, as I prepared this perfect sacrificial lamb for burial, that the Father's message in the Law of Moses was this: None of us can keep the law. The sacrifice for our failures, for our sins, was right there all along.

When Moses received the law, all of the sacrifices were right there with all of the laws. Our Father knew (he made us, after all) we would strive to be perfect and fail. He gave us freedom and knew that in our arrogance and attempts to appear what we were not that we would need to be cleansed.

I had spent most of my life trying to perfect myself, to not need a sacrifice, and now, I loved the sacrifice. I gently scrubbed the caked blood from the body the Son used while he walked—next to me and everyone else. What a glorious sacrifice. What an honor to be in the presence of this final and perfect Lamb.

---

[39] John 3:7, 8.

It is like the wind. The Spirit, I am beginning to perceive, is all around us, but unless we quiet ourselves, we can miss it. I nearly did.

But I will no longer. I will attune myself to the wind of the Spirit. In this moment, on this table of death, the man-God-Messiah answered my question to the full. What is most important? How can I be saved? How can I be perfect in holiness?

I peeled a row of thorns from the bloody forehead of the final sacrifice; he has answered.

The voice of the Lamb rolls on the wind.

It is finished.[40]

Praise God. It is finished.

UNPACKING NICODEMUS AND THE WIND

The Pharisees are easy prey.

We can so easily take apart their legalism and ugliness because even the scripture does it for us.

Honestly, though, I am a recovering Pharisee.

How about you?

I was raised in a faith system that was very works-oriented, legalistic, and transactional. The Pharisees came to our system of faith with all good intentions. Pharisees may appear ugly but are just responding to the insecurity and fear of trying to do what we can only do through the grace, power, and mercy of God Almighty.

We all wanted to take the Word of God seriously and be pleasing to the Lord. We wanted to oppose false teaching so no one would be led astray. We (and the Pharisees) all had noble intent.

But the fruit, once again, tends to be on the rotten (ungodly)

---

40 John 19:30.

side. Let's look at some lessons from Nicodemus, Yeshua, and the faith of the Pharisees (and modern-day Pharisees):

SENSING THE WIND

The Good News (the Gospel) is such great news that we have trouble accepting it, and so we do not.

Most of our lives, amongst people just like us, we experience a transactional form of living. In other words, if you are nice to me, I'll be nice to you. If you do something good for me, I'll do something good for you. If you forget me this Christmas, I'll stop giving you gifts next Christmas (since I gave you one this year). These are examples of transactional living.

It is the most common form of love in our world, and it is natural that we take this into our relationship with the Messiah without even meaning to.

Legalistic systems of faith take the words of Jesus, "If you love me, you will keep my commandments," and invert them. This verse was brought up frequently in my early faith system as to why you must strive so diligently to keep all the New Testament commands. Because if Jesus is going to be able to love you, you must show him you love him by keeping all of his commandments.

The first thing wrong with this view (which I held for much of my early life in Christ, into my young adult years) is that it inverts what Jesus said and corrupts what he intended.

He did not say, "Keep my commandments, and if you do, then I'll know you love me, and then I might love you (since you're so awesome at commandment-keeping)."

The love for him comes first.

58

A friend of mine put it best. He grew up on a farm and was "volun-told" to participate in all of the animal care that went along with that.

As a result, he does not care for animals in his house, his life, or even in the yard. The ultimate freedom of his adult life would be found in not having animals at all. Ever.

He has animals in his house. Dogs, birds, cats, and who knows what else will come to reside with him.

Why? Because he loves his wife, and she adores animals.

He loves his wife, so he does for her what speaks love to her heart, without objection.

He brings animals into his house, out of love for his wife.

The love came first, then the animals.

Do you get the difference?

If I love Jesus (and I do), I will seek to know him increasingly as he is, as I walk through life with him, and because I love him, I will do those things pretty much naturally that are reflective of his beautiful heart.

So no, we don't keep commands to qualify us to be loved by God.

Further, what are the commands of Christ?

You need to answer this on your own, but here's the secret decoder ring for you and a starter answer.

A command is given in such a way that all covenantal people get it, and it is in the form of a "do this/don't do that" type of wording. With Jesus (or his apostles, who had the authority to bind things as they taught by the Spirit), you are looking for something like "You shall love the Lord your God with all your heart and with all your soul and with all your mind. This is the great and first commandment. And a second is like it: You shall love your neighbor as yourself. On these two commandments depend all the Law and the Prophets."

It is remarkable and noteworthy that in these two commandments, Jesus basically says you can summarize all the old law: that is, love God and love others.

In my faith tradition growing up, we would speak of the formal-worship commands, which would be typified by someone saying, "We are commanded to sing." We believed that Ephesian 5:17–21 and Colossians 3:12–17 were commandments to sing.

There is one problem: These verses are not commands, but rather admonishments. One of the cardinal rules of biblical interpretation is to never read just one Bible verse. In other words, you need to back up and see what is being talked about before you can even understand the verse. The passage in Ephesians is preceded by a "therefore"; the one in Colossians is introduced by a "then" (in the ESV; your Bible may choose a different English term), but this clearly makes these qualify as admonishments, wise things to do in view of what is being discussed. Further, is a concept of formal worship even mentioned in the New Testament?

Worship isn't just something we do when we come together as believers; it is also what I do every waking moment as I walk with my Lord and the Holy Spirit, every minute of every day. When you love someone who is as totally wonderful and lovable as Yeshua, the Son of God, you just naturally do everything for him. What is of his heart becomes what your heart values, because of the love relationship between you.

After all, in our baptism, we died to ourselves and were raised as new creatures, with new vision and priorities. In the words of Jesus to our friend Nicodemus, we were born again. Our relationship is anything but transactional; it is completely love-based, as the apostle Paul says so well:

> But God, being rich in mercy, because of the great love with which he loved us, even when we were dead in our trespasses, made us alive together with Christ—by grace you have been saved—and raised us up with him and seated us with him in the heavenly places in Christ Jesus, so that in the coming ages he might show the immeasurable riches of his grace in kindness toward us in Christ Jesus. For by grace you have been saved through faith. And this is not your own doing; it is the gift of God, not as a result of works, so that no one may boast.[41]

As mere mortals walking in a transactional world, this is truly hard to accept.

Embrace the wind of grace and the Spirit.

TAKEAWAY 1: In order to truly accept the good news, we must be attuned to spiritual realities. As Jesus pointed out to Nicodemus, this requires we purposely sense the wind of the Spirit and of the grace, mercy, and beauty of our Lord. The good news is unnatural; it is supernatural. We struggle to accept it, but until we do, we will be lacking in joy.

---

[41] Ephesians 2:4–9.

SYSTEMS DO NOT SAVE

The Pharisees had a system of faith, what we might call a "creed" or "statement of faith" today. Those are okay (perhaps), but we are saved by the Savior and not by a system. We must focus on the Savior.

If you study the history of various reformation/restoration movements, you will find at their root a desire for greater faithfulness to scripture, but at some point, there is a perceived need to have everyone believe and follow the same system of faith. This (supposedly) is to prevent apostasy or heresy, but it also assumes that an infallible doctrine has already been achieved. That is a bold assumption, lacking humility.

The Pharisees were very dedicated to following scripture, so much so they added a barrier of protective laws on top of the laws in order to avoid sinning against God.

But even the old law was handed down with the sacrifices enclosed, God telling us that without him and a provision for cleansing, no one would survive.

No one.

There is no need for a barrier of protective anything because the perfect Lamb has already been offered.

The old law (and even elements predating the old law) prophesied that the ultimate and final sacrifice would one day arrive. The perfect lamb would die for all; what was needed was not a series of yearly sacrifices (and certainly not perfect law-keeping) but a final and complete substitutionary sacrifice for all of us as sinners. We know him most commonly by the transliterated name Jesus, but his Hebrew given name was *Yeshua* ("Joshua" in English terms). He was the anointed one of God (Messiah) and was the only suitable sacrifice for all of us. It is finished. A Savior who saves us, not a system.

> **TAKEAWAY 2:** We need a Savior, not a system, in order to reach our eternal destiny with our Creator God. A system of faith must be open to being examined in light of scripture. Listen to the critics of your system of faith; is your system humble and changeable?

FEAR PRODUCES SLAVERY

Systems of faith are founded in the fear of humans. Perfect love casts out fear.

My wife and I visited a beautiful old church while on vacation in Bar Harbor, Maine. They were holding a concert for the public. As we sat in the pews, I noticed a thick book and pulled it out of the songbook holder. I was amazed.

It had the words written out for every kind of prayer, statements to be made (verbatim) for someone taking a church "office" (their words), a marriage, and just about anything else you could imagine.

It was a product of fear, raw fear. Someone might say something differently from the way the ones with perfect knowledge knew it should be done. That, of course, would be unacceptable. But of course, no one outside of our Holy God has perfect knowledge; knowing God perfectly will take, oh, maybe an eternity with him.

'Nuff said?

> **TAKEAWAY 3:** "The fear of man lays a snare, but whoever trusts in the Lord is safe" (Proverbs 29:25). Your system of faith may have a long and well-documented history; that does not mean it is right in God's sight.

LEARN TO LIVE IN THE SPIRIT

There is a truth Jesus told Nicodemus that does not sit well with linear, logical, and self-powered believers: Yeah, it's the wind thing.

I perceive that what Nicodemus really wanted to hear was what he was missing in all of his diligent efforts to please God.

To paraphrase Jesus's answer, Nicodemus needed to get in touch with the most real thing about us and the world around us (and so do we). We are spiritual creatures with a temporary body. There is, raging around us, a spiritual battle in which the army of the Lord (angelic beings) are fighting with and for us, while the forces of Satan are engaged in battle against us and the angelic host of the army of the Lord.

Living in the Spirit requires us to calm ourselves, to spend time in the Word with its author, to reflect, and to perceive what needs to happen spiritually.

We must become more perceptive to the wind-like nature of spiritual reality. We must know all the Bible with increasing familiarity, in order to discern the voice of the Spirit. That is because, as we just mentioned about the spiritual battle, the Holy Spirit is not the only spiritual being out there. I keep pounding this truth home and will continue to do so, but if you consider yourself to be led by the Spirit but do not spend copious amounts of time dwelling in the Word—you are in dangerous territory.

If you hear something you think is from the Holy Spirit of God that contradicts who God has already revealed himself to be in the Word, you are not Spirit-led, you are spirit-led. Maybe it is Satan, or maybe it is your own selfish spirit, but it cannot be from God. The Spirit will never contradict revealed truth.

TAKEAWAY 4: Regarding the wind and hearing from the Spirit, dwell in the revealed Word of God so you can recognize truth when the Spirit speaks to you. Learn to be sensitive to the wind-like impressions and leading of the Holy Spirit.

FOLLOWING JESUS MAY COST YOU

Seeing and following Christ may require you to stand against the teachings accepted by your faith group, and it may be costly.

Nicodemus begins to step out a bit in John 7:50. The Pharisees were trying to arrest Jesus but having a lot of trouble getting anyone to do it. Nicodemus asks an important question: "Does our law judge a man without first giving him a hearing and learning what he does?"

Nicodemus is clearly considering that Jesus may be who he claims, and he is hopeful that his fellow Jews will slow down and consider the evidence.

It doesn't go well for him.

They respond with a fallacy: "Are you from Galilee too?"[42]

---

[42] John 7:52.

This is the famous ad hominem fallacy, which means to attack the man. Nicodemus brings up a valid point from the law; they respond by saying even considering what the Nazarene rabbi is doing or saying is to be a "Galilean," or an incompetent fool. They did not answer his objection; they just accused him of being uneducated.

If you find your church family upholding something scripturally wrong, gently reprove and rebuke them. If they counterattack instead of sitting and discussing things from scripture, then it may be time to shake the dust off your feet.

I've seen this done in my community, where an entire church voted to leave the denominational headquarters they were under because of unbiblical mandates from said group. It was bold, it was godly, and it was the right thing to do.

I suspect that after Nicodemus helped bury Jesus, his council days were over. If he hadn't already torn his robe, he likely had to turn it in—along with his membership card.

Regardless, I suspect that Nicodemus was full of joy.

TAKEAWAY 5: Following the Messiah may require you to stand up for truth (humbly) and could result in you having to go elsewhere.

Chapter Four

THE MAN WITH LIVING WATER

The Woman at the Well

Every day is like the other now. Hot, sad, and lonely.

The heat in this little mud-brick house is rising, but there is no place nearby that's any cooler.

I looked down at Silas. He was snoring on the straw pallet, even though the sun was high in the sky. He had come home very late, very drunk, and I had greeted him with my usual charm. I accused him of not caring about me and of running with the prostitutes in town.

My voice, oh, my voice was shrill and harsh. I'm surprised he hasn't kicked me out by now.

Why am I so angry now? Yeah, well, why wouldn't I be angry? Life has been one bitter moment after another.

For all his faults, Silas is at least gentle. Or maybe he's just passive. Life had been hard for him too. Maybe that was the only thing in life we both shared, besides this little dumpy house.

67

He had taken me in a year ago when I was once again living on the streets. Was it pity? Or just his loneliness? It's not that he was really handsome or successful; I was just relieved that he seemed to care that I was hurting. I was happier for a short time, but then, I went back to my old, angry, and critical spirit. I'm not sure why he puts up with me. I don't even like me anymore.

I looked out through the tattered remains of the cloth door to this house. The heat rising off the ground distorted everything, and there wasn't much to see around here. We lived a bit of a walk from Sychar; it was rocky and barren.

Barren; kind of fits me.

It was good to be away from the town in some ways—to be away from the condescending stares of the people, the hands clasped over the mouths, whispering about me when they saw me.

Two days ago, I had dared to feel good again. I went to town to trade some animal skins Silas had prepared. As I walked toward the marketplace, I saw my childhood friend, Anna, walking with a younger woman. Strange, I had never seen the girl before, but then I had been avoiding town for a while. Maybe she moved here?

When I saw Anna, I was feeling good and smiled at my old friend and the new girl. What was I thinking?

Anna quickly covered her mouth and whispered something to the young lady, and she looked shocked and then turned away.

"Thanks for making sure everyone knows how messed up I am," I said to no one but me. Even a simple trip to town magnified my pain and reminded me of my failures.

I choked back the tears. I needed to be strong to negotiate as much food or cloth as I could with what I had; everyone knew me in town. And that was the problem.

I jolted back to reality when Silas suddenly snorted—breaking the regular loud snoring that sounded something like the noise a camel makes when it is angry. He rolled to his other side and went back to sleep, but he would be awake soon.

I looked into the water pot; it was nearly empty. I was thirsty, but I didn't dare drink. I carefully poured the last of the water into Silas's cup. He would be thirsty when he woke up, and I didn't want to be on the streets again. I suspected Silas was tiring of my company.

I was tired of my company.

I often thought of leaving, but where would I go? It was hard being a woman in Samaria, especially a woman on her own. I remember the first divorce, my first time being homeless. I had just had my second miscarriage, still bleeding. He had gone to the priest and put me away. I remember crying myself to sleep under a bush, too hungry and weak to even seek food or water. I almost died then; I almost died.

Too bad I hadn't.

I pulled through and lived out in the open. I remember sneaking into a garden and spending two beautiful days sleeping next to some of the most beautiful flowers I had ever seen.

The garden.

My abba always had been a farmer, and his garden was so gorgeous. We would plant, weed, and harvest together. It was a magical place for me: the smells, the colors, the time spent with my father. We would sneak some of the early fruit and vegetables off the plants and eat in the shade of the olive trees.

Why had he died so soon?

I felt the intense sadness coming on. I can't go there. I have to get water. It was the middle of the day, when no one went to the well. The women all got water in the morning or just before the sun set. It was cooler then, but I was definitely not welcome amongst the women of Sychar. Now was the time for me. I would have to take the long rocky walk to the well. I was already thirsty, and the pot was heavy, but at least I could drink my fill at the well, which was good, since the pot would be much heavier on the trip back.

I looked at the water jar. It was the only thing I had left from my mother. And it had belonged to my grandmother. But it was showing its age. It had several chips around the upper lip, and a crack had appeared that went from the top diagonally to the midsection. When I filled it up, it would begin seeping water, slowly seeping down upon me so that by the time I got home, at least a third of it was gone.

Yes, it was less than perfect, but it was at least a connection with my mother. She had not done well after my abba had died. She was beautiful, and I had been her only child. She had several miscarriages. For some reason, I had lived; that was good, I guess. She loved me, but she was very sad. My abba tried to cheer her up, always telling her how beautiful she was and how she was the Lord's special blessing to him. He adored her so much. But she seemed to take the miscarriages as her own fault.

And as much as she tried to love me, I think she felt she had failed my abba. It was the best of women who provided boys for their husbands; Mama had given birth to three boys, but none of them lived more than a week. My abba didn't care, and he made that clear. He loved his "girls," as he called both of us. He truly treasured and was thrilled by the two of us.

But Mama always felt ashamed; she saw the other women with

their families, the boys walking right behind their abba in town, a constant reminder of how she had let down the man she loved.

I tried to be silly and cheer her up, but it hurt me inside to see her face. She was so beautiful, yet the lines from her sad face had grown deep. She looked older than she was. When Abba or I made her laugh, her smile lit up the room.

I think she had died of sadness.

I picked up the old water jar and pushed through the door. I hadn't gone far before I thought about going back and drinking the last cup of water; the sun was hitting me hard, and I wasn't feeling too well already. I didn't want to give Silas any more reasons to kick me out, though. He kept insisting I was always welcome in his house, and that it was our home. But for some reason, I couldn't believe that. Every other man got rid of me. I stopped and looked back, thinking of the water, but I turned and started up the rocky hill toward the well. I could make it.

The walk was hard and uneven, and it going to be even harder when the jar was full of water on the way back. But at least I could drink my fill at the well. My mouth was already dry, and my clothes felt hot against my skin. There was no wind today; it was dead still. It felt foreboding, like something bad was going to happen. I could sense something was awaiting me.

My heart was racing, and I was breathing hard when I reached the top of the first hill. I stopped and looked around; it was so desolate. It looked like what I felt inside. Hot tears were rolling down my face; why was life so hard for me?

My old friends, they all married, had children; some even had grandchildren. Why not me? Oh, I had been with child a few times, felt the child kick, and even held my still-warm baby in my arms, but none lived. But none lived; my tears came on stronger. Why does God let my children die? Was it too much to ask for one living child?

I talked to my God, looking toward the sky. I listened but heard nothing. What good is this God, who does not show me love? Does he even know me? Does he care that I am empty and dead inside?

I was coming down the first hill now. There was a small tree at the bottom. I picked up my pace a bit to make it to the shade. I was beginning to feel dizzy and too hot.

I made it and sat down in the sparse shade. I was panting and covered in sweat. I carefully set my mother's jar in front of me and lay back onto the rocky ground. As I closed my eyes, I noticed a familiar scent; I had smelled this before. It was something from long ago: my abba's garden.

This tree, or bush, yes, my abba had many of these in his garden. It had beautiful violet flowers in the spring. He loved his garden, and I loved my abba. My abba loved me. We worked together preparing the soil, planting, pruning, and eating from his garden. It was our special place. Both of us escaped the sadness of my mother when we were in his garden. We would taste the ripened fruit and giggle with delight. My abba would chase me and grab me up, tickling me, and the joy I would see in his eyes every time he looked at me; why did he see me so differently?

Did anyone else like seeing me?

I stared at the pot in front of me. In the sun, it looked even more worn and old.

I picked it up, stood up, and continued toward the well.

The pot wasn't the only thing showing its age.

I had caught a reflection of myself last week, after an unexpected heavy rain. There was a wadi near Silas's house, and it was full of smooth, calm water. The sun was low and illuminated my face in the water.

I had been very pretty in earlier years; I had easily attracted husbands in the past. But what I saw last week brought fear; I saw an older-looking woman. My hair was ragged and graying; lines of sadness were beginning to show on my face. I was becoming my mama. I didn't have a funny little girl or my abba to cheer me up. I was completely alone, unloved. I was wearing my pain on my face.

Would Silas kick me out soon? I had better start smiling and stop criticizing. I don't know if I could take another year alone in Sychar.

No one could love me; I didn't even like me.

Silas was surely going to get rid of me.

Why couldn't I be lovable? Was there a man out there who would smile with joy when he saw me, like my abba?

Every time he saw me, it was like he saw some great prize. He would scoop me up in his arms and squeeze me. He would tell me what he had done in town that day, the deals he had made, the people he had laughed with. And at night, he would tell me of the God he loved and lived for. He would speak of the Messiah who would someday come and who would even heal the great hatred between us Samaritans and the Jews. We would be brothers and sisters again, living together with love when the Messiah came.

Where was this God of my abba? I just couldn't feel the love for this God that my father had felt. Where was he? Why did he hate me? Why had God forsaken me?

The second hill was harder than the first. Where was this Messiah when you needed him? Was he even real? Does he know how hard and sad my life is? Would he care about me, a sinful woman?

Or was the Messiah just a happy story abbas told their children to give hope?

Hope?

There probably is no Messiah; if he is real, he wouldn't care for me. I completely messed up my life; was there a command I hadn't broken?

My abba made me feel like I was beautiful and worthy just because I was his Salome.

Those days were long gone.

I didn't have much to offer anyone anymore. What could I give to Messiah?

I reached the top of the second hill; the well wasn't too far beyond that. But I felt very hot, and I had stopped sweating. I stopped just short of the crest, still breathing hard. I might not make it. I felt a sudden terror.

I might not make it; I lowered my jar to the ground.

I felt suddenly calm.

I might not make it.

Death would be better than life. My whole life, what was it worth? I lived with Silas, but I was so alone. How could he love a barren woman who complained to him daily? I wasn't pretty; I wasn't fun. He carried most of the weight, other than water.

Water: At least that would feel good. I picked up my mother's jar; it felt heavier than ever. I slowly moved toward the top of the hill. I felt dizzy and stumbled. I wasn't sure if I could go on. Then I imagined the feel of the always-cool well water, the way it refreshed you from the inside out. I thought about how good it would feel to jump in the water during the spring rains. I looked up; the cloudless sky mocked my dreams.

Nobody would be there to see me waste the water. Yes, this would be good. I would pour the first jar full over me and just lay down in the shade of the little shelter next to the well.

I reached the top and looked down the trail; I saw the well, but was someone sitting there?

It was hard to see because of the heat; my vision seemed to be greying a bit, but someone was sitting in the little shelter at the well. There were no animals, no other people, just a lone man sitting at the well.

Great.

That's all I need today, of all days. More stares of condemnation. He probably heard about me. "Here's the sinner, the adulterer, that woman." The tears flowed heavily again. Apparently, I still had a little water in my dried-out body. I paused, but then I felt my anger rising.

So be it. Why would I let some man direct my path? What favors had any man ever done for me? I started down the path with more life in my step than when I had started. I was still dizzy, but I no longer cared. If I die, that's good. If this proud man gives me one wrong look, I'll let him know what I think.

But then as I walked, I thought of the beautiful face of my smiling abba.

Not all men are bad.

His love was full, beautiful, and life-giving.

He had given me life and made my life beautiful.

We weren't rich, and life in Sychar was hard, but I felt rich, and when I was with my abba, I always felt light and fast. I felt beautiful and loved. If someone else treated me bad, I ran to him. He always loved me, he always understood me, and nothing I messed up could stand between my abba and me.

Except that he died.

For nine years, I was the queen of Samaria; at least that's what I felt like.

Why had God taken him from me so soon? Is there a God somewhere? Why would a God not be more like my abba and see me with joy?

I looked up again; I was close to the well, and my heart sank.

It wasn't a man from Sychar; no, his clothing told the story.

It was someone special, at least in his mind.

It was a Jew.

A stinking Jew.

Yeah, where was this Messiah when you needed him? I needed him now. Where was this Savior to beat this arrogant Jew and run him from the well?

As if the men of Sychar wouldn't wear me out for who I was, for my past. This Jew would have double condemnation for me. Not only was I a Samaritan, a half-breed, and a traitor to the Jewish people, but I was also just a woman. I was a dog to the dogs.

That's just great.

I stopped for a moment and looked back from where I had come. I couldn't go back. I wasn't sure I'd have the strength to pull the water out of the well now, and then I looked back at the man at the well. He was looking at me already, no doubt clicking his tongue in disgust.

I felt the return of my rage. Sometimes my rage was useful.

I was going to get my water, drink all I wanted, and even pour the first jar all over me. I wouldn't even make eye contact with him until I was soaking wet, and then I would laugh at him and say, "Oh, sorry, are you thirsty?" Or maybe, "Shocking how my body looks all wet, huh, Jew?"

I moved forward, and I could sense he was staring straight at me. I tried to just look at my feet, but then I just had to steal a glance to confirm. I cut my eyes in his direction, just briefly.

He was smiling at me; why?

He was very ordinary looking, and his face was friendly. His smile; I quickly looked back, and it stirred something inside of me. I felt faint.

The way he looked at me, why was it so familiar?

I had to get the water and go. I felt suddenly nervous, dizzy, and still so thirsty. I would just get my water and go. I could drink when I got back over the hill.

Why was he looking at me that way?

I made it to the well, nearly falling as I knelt down with my jar. I was very weak and struggled to uncover the well. I turned my head slightly; I could see the man still sitting on one of the large rocks to the side; it looked like he was wiping away a tear.

No, probably just the dust; why would a Jew shed a tear for a lowly Samaritan woman?

I attached the hook to my jar and lowered it quickly to the water below and began pulling it up. It seemed heavier than ever, and my vision was blurring. I was feeling very weak.

I barely got the now-heavy jar back to the ground and was panting again, like the Samaritan dog I was. My self-condemnation was suddenly interrupted, and it felt like my heart nearly stoppped.

"Give me a drink."[43]

What? Oh, how typical for a Jewish man. Here I am struggling, hot, and about to pass out, and all he can do is ask me to serve him? How inconsiderate; he could have at least helped me pull the jar up.

I stared at the old jar; my jaw was tight. I ground my teeth together so hard, I thought they would crack.

I could sense the man still staring at me.

Here I had walked all this way, I'm so weak, and I'm doing all the work. "Give me a drink?" I haven't even had a drink yet.

I found some restraint somewhere within me; I guess I was a little afraid of Jews, in spite of my inner rage.

"How is it that you, a Jew, ask for a drink from me, a woman of Samaria?"[44] I heard myself say, my voice cracking and dry. It wasn't really what I wanted to say, but I hoped he would get the message: Get your own water, you arrogant fool.

He was quiet.

I turned my head slightly and lifted my eyes to him.

He sat with his head slightly turned; his face looked very gentle, and tears were rolling down his cheeks as he spoke: "If you knew the gift of God, and who it is that is saying to you, 'Give me a drink,' you would have asked him, and he would have given you living water."[45]

I looked back at my jar. I felt so confused; why the tears? What does this even mean? He's going to give me water?

I felt my rage rise again; oh, no, he's messing with my mind. This is the magical Jewish moment, where he humiliates me. This

---

[43] John 4:7.

[44] John 4:9.

[45] Ibid., v. 10.

haughty man who is so superior to me, he claims he can produce water out of thin, hot, and very dry air. The boldness of this guy, all while producing a fake tear, or was it just sweat?

Yes, that was it. He's just sweaty and needing water.

I looked back. I'm sure my anger was showing on my face, and he was smiling? He was looking at me like—I heard my voice, a bit sarcastic, say:

"Sir, you have nothing to draw water with, and the well is deep. Where do you get that living water? Are you greater than our father Jacob? He gave us the well and drank from it himself, his sons, and his livestock."[46]

I hoped he got the message, a reminder that I came from the same family as he did. I didn't get to choose that my forefathers were trapped here; I had no choice as to who I was born. How dare these Jews think themselves more worthy just because of something I had no control over? Jacob was a good Jew, and so am I. Maybe that will shut him up.

I picked up my jar and stood, unsteadily; time was wasting, and the water was already leaking from the jar. I nearly tripped with my first steps; I really needed a drink. I needed to rest. *Get your own stinking water, you lousy Jew.*

I walked past the man back toward Silas's home.

"Everyone who drinks of this water will be thirsty again, but whoever drinks of the water I give him will never be thirsty again. The water that I will give him will become in him a spring of water welling up to eternal life."[47]

I stopped walking. My rage had quickly returned. The same

---

[46] John 4:11, 12.

[47] Ibid., vv. 13, 14.

rage that would probably put me on the streets again when Silas saw me for who I really was.

I turned to face the man straight on, bent over, and slammed my jar down hard on the ground. Water sloshed over the sides and onto the dust below.

"Sir, give me this water, so that I will not be thirsty or have to come here to draw water."[48]

My face had to be ugly, defiant, and showing the contempt I felt for this man. I was pointing at the well, and tears were flowing down my face. I challenged him to produce this mystical water— this arrogant and no-good tormentor.

He shook his head agreeably and said with absolute gentleness, "Go, call your husband, and come here."[49]

All my defiance left me. Why hadn't I kept my bitter mouth shut?

I looked down, hesitating. I didn't know what to say. I bent over, picked up the heavy water, and turned toward the hill, but I was now so weak. I stopped, turned my head slightly, and answered softly, "I, um, have no husband."[50]

I slowly started walking, hoping I could escape. I didn't need any more pain today. I stopped and looked up the long hill, unsure if I could—

"You are right in saying, 'I have no husband'; for you have had five husbands, and the one you have now is not your husband."[51]

---

[48] John 4:15.
[49] Ibid., v. 16.
[50] Ibid., v. 17.
[51] Ibid., vv. 17, 18.

My feet stopped; I had never felt so completely naked in my entire life.

I set my jar down by my feet, and it toppled over, and I heard a sharp sound as the pot fractured along the old crack. The water washed over the dusty ground. My tears began flowing like I didn't know they could, and my knees collapsed. I fell to the ground and sobbed.

I turned myself awkwardly on my knees and looked back at the man.

His face was full of pain—my pain? He said in the gentlest voice, "What you have said is true."[52]

His voice was so kind. I felt as though my heart was going to explode. I looked back at the broken jar, the water still dribbling out. I felt like the jar. I was done. My tears were hitting the dust and making small little clouds.

I looked back at the man, the way he was looking at me, it was just so—

"Sir, I perceive that you are prophet,"[53] I heard a voice say. It was me, but it was weak and quiet. My defiance, rage, and indignation were fading.

His eyes lit up, and he smiled a beautiful smile at me—about me?

I recalled the words of my father, stirred by the smile and eyes of this mysterious man; there was one coming who would know all things and make things right. My heart felt a hope, and I had not felt this for a very long time. This couldn't be, but he knew me. He still looked at me like my—

---

[52] Ibid.

[53] John 4:19.

Could my father have been right? I heard my voice once again speaking, quietly, trembling, yet expectantly:

"Our fathers worshiped on this mountain, but you say that in Jerusalem is the place where people ought to worship."[54]

He gently replied, "Woman, believe me, the hour is coming when neither on this mountain nor in Jerusalem will you worship the Father. You worship what you do not know; we worship what we know, for salvation is from the Jews. But the hour is coming, and is now here, when the true worshipers will worship the Father in spirit and truth, for the Father is seeking such people to worship him. God is spirit, and those who worship him must worship in spirit and truth."[55]

I heard it; could it be? He said, "The hour is ... now here"? Could this be?

My heart was racing; I had to say it, though my hopes had been crushed for so long. Could this be? My thoughts raced back to the promises my abba had told me from the Holy Words. I had to say it. My voice was timid; I sounded like I did when I was a scared little girl.

"I know that Messiah is coming (he who is called Christ). When he comes, he will tell us all things."[56]

I stared now into his kind face, for the first time in a long time speaking to God in my own head: *Please let this be him.*

He nodded his head, smiling that smile I had last seen on my abba, who loved me like no one else.

---

54 Ibid., 4:20.
55 Ibid., vv. 21–24.
56 John 4:25.

"I who speak to you am he."[57]

I burst out laughing, then clasped my hands over my mouth—should I laugh if it is he? I bowed to the ground. My heart was racing again, and I could smell the dust of the ground. How did he know about all my life, my husbands? Why did he look at me in the same way my father did? He had to be—

I heard footsteps approaching, and suddenly a gentle set of hands raised me up. He held my face, smiled, and said, "Salome, shalom." I suddenly felt energized, like I had just drank my fill of the sweetest water; I felt cool and alive. Living water! Yes, living water; it was him. I stared into his eyes and saw nothing but love, compassion, and joy—for me?

He hugged me tightly; I hadn't been hugged that way since—

I noticed a group of Jewish men had arrived and surrounded us; they looked very shocked. I pulled back from this man of love, the Messiah.

I looked at these Jewish men, pointed at the Messiah, and yelled, "It's him! It's him. He knows all. And He loves me."

The man, the Messiah, he was laughing harder than anyone. His eyes were bright, and he was nodding yes, he loves me. Yes, he is the Messiah.

I turned and began to run toward town. I looked back again, and the Messiah was still laughing, watching, and shooing me on toward town. I felt light and happy, and as I began seeing the people from my town, I grabbed them and yelled, "I have found Messiah. He is at the well; he knows all things."

I heard my father's laughter, and I knew I was loved; the Messiah.

---

[57] Ibid., v. 26.

UNPACKING THE WOMAN AT THE WELL AND JESUS

The story of how Jesus walked straight into Samaria and loved a lost woman is incredibly relevant to our situation today. With all of the claims of oppression, intersectionality, and privilege, Jesus helps us to straighten our path and love as he would love.

COME TO JESUS AS YOU ARE

Jesus loves you with a reckless love. You are his creation, his delight.

Life can be brutal, and in the midst of that, we can really make a mess of things. We can experience the loss of those we love the most, face rejection by those who promise a lifetime of faithfulness, and be ostracized by those around us because of what they know (or think they know) about us.

Jesus loves you. You do not have to straighten up your mess in order to be in a saving and gracious relationship with him, just trust that what he did on the cross was more than enough to save you from your sins.

Further, do not think he wants you to stay enslaved in your sin; he stands beside you with his arms around you, saying, "I see your big pile of mess, and we'll work on that together whenever you are ready."

TAKEAWAY 1: Yeshua (Jesus) the Christ is not waiting for you to get your act together; he is ready to accept you, and as you come to know and love him, you will naturally seek to do what pleases him. Accept the "riches of his grace which he lavished upon"[58] you; find your worth in him and in his people (his called-out ones, his church).

EVERY PERSON BEARS THE IMAGE OF GOD

Jesus gave no attention to the racial or oppressive ideologies of his day, and neither should we.

It was normal for Jews traveling where Jesus was going to be very careful to not soil their feet with Samaritan dust. The hatred was strong. The Samaritans deserved mistreatment because of the supposed impurity of previous generations and some wrong done by the same. Jesus walks straight into Samaria and receives a Samaritan woman as a sister or daughter, loving her and providing for her what she needed most.

In other words, he treats her as what she is. She is a precious creature who bears the image of God. Period. What people of her identity group did or any supposed impurity of her people (what might be called "race" today) does not change anything in the love Jesus shows for her.

Enough said?

---

[58] Ephesian 1:7, 8.

> **TAKEAWAY 2:** Be to all others as Jesus was to the Samaritan woman. Be loving, be accepting, be understanding, and thereby give them what your Lord has lavished upon you. Do not treat others poorly because of something their supposed identity group did in the past; each of us is a beautiful image-bearer of our amazing God.

LET GOD WORK THROUGH YOU

Your life may have been a hot sinful mess up to now, and you may be hated by those around you, but you can start a spiritual revolution through the power of the one who loves and lives in you.

"Many Samaritans believed in him because of the woman's testimony," says John 4:39. When this woman, who likely had no respect amongst her neighbors, encountered the beauty and grace of the Messiah, she was unstoppable.

In fact, she started a spiritual revolution in her town.

The power of the Good News, or the Gospel, is not found in us; it is found in he who abides in us. The woman at the well shared her joy about the man who knew her yet loved her. She recognized in him a supernatural knowledge and correctly believed he was the anointed one scripture had pointed toward for centuries.

In her joy in the Christ, she was an unstoppable force for spreading the Gospel.

You can be too.

TAKEAWAY 3: Your internal voice and the voice of those around you may make you feel powerless. But the abiding of Jesus and the Holy Spirit in you are where the power lies. Just as the Samaritan woman changed her village, so can you, if you abide in the love of Christ in faith.

Chapter Five

FIXING THE ONE-TRICK PONY

The Crippled Man at the Pool of Bethesda

Do I want to be healed?

I couldn't believe he even asked. I was all at once furious, confused, shocked, and ashamed.

Maybe the shame took a while to hit me. Something inside of me was exposed the moment this man walked out of nowhere and singled me out. I was by no means the only person with a problem sitting by that supposedly magical healing pool called Bethesda.[59]

It was just another day sitting in the afternoon shade on that patio. There were advantages to being there. Many of the Jewish women, especially the old mothers who had no one left to care for, would come by with food and even gifts. They would sit and talk; we would share food sometimes, and they would talk about their kids and grandkids.

At this point, I thought kids were way past a possibility, but here

---

[59] The story of this man is found in John 5.

I was, three kids and a wife. And that after spending thirty-eight years wallowing in helplessness.

Did I want to be healed?

So there I was, just sitting in the shade next to the pool.

Well, not really next to it, exactly; I had learned where to sit to get warmed by the sun in the cool of the morning, but to be in the shade during the heat of the day. That also was where all the older ladies liked to sit, since they usually came later in the day. I had staked out a prime seat; I would glare at anyone who dared to take my spot.

Did I want to get better? My official answer would have always been, absolutely yes.

But that day, when the rabbi from Nazareth suddenly stood over me, asking, "Do you want to be healed?"[60] that was the beginning of my real life.

It was scary, but I discovered that for the previous three decades, I had been hiding in fear, and that is no way to live.

This Yeshua, the regular guy from Nazareth, he knew.

He knew where I was, better than I knew myself. It's amazing how we can deceive not only others, but our own hearts.

I couldn't deceive the Messiah.

When he asked me if I wanted to be healed, I did feel completely undone, but I also felt the need to say something. I think I replied something like, "Sir, I have no one to put me into the pool when the water is stirred up, and while I am going down another steps down before me."[61]

I guess that was sort of true, at one time.

---

[60] John 5:6.
[61] Ibid., v. 7.

The first time my family had taken me to the patio by the healing pool, I was a young man. We had heard some people claim to have been healed, and that sounded good. My family took me down there and stayed when they could, but the pool didn't stir at convenient times. Everyone had to work to stay alive, and everyone had to work a bit extra to keep me alive. At first, I felt kind of bad about that, but later—

The first few times I saw the pool bubbling, I delayed. It wasn't as dramatic as I thought it would be, more of just a rising than some miraculous thing, and someone did beat me into the water. By that point, I was pretty much just dragging myself by my arms.

I got more serious and learned to recognize the rising of the pool and tried to get in a few times but was never the first.

Strange thing is, those who were first didn't really seem to get fully healed.

They would be perhaps more energized, more excited, and more mobile for a while, but it wasn't what I would call a complete healing.

Sitting close to the pool for hours every day, sometimes not seeing a stirring for weeks on end, was tiring and hot.

I tried a few different places to be more comfortable and also learned how to draw the attention (and food) of the old ladies.

To be honest, I had found my niche. I was the nice cripple, so understanding and enjoyable for the ladies to talk to. They felt sorry for me, and I was attentive and good for them.

Did I want to be healed?

He knew.

I was comfortable. I had the attention of my brothers; I didn't have to worry about working or getting hurt (hey, I was already on the injured list), and a lot of people went out of their way to show me sympathy and give me things.

In fact, I had more people who knew me than both of my brothers put together.

Did I really want to be healed?

No.

On that day, when Yeshua looked me in the eyes, something pierced the hardened crust around my heart. He didn't really seem to have any regard for my weak answer about having no one to help; he just said, "Get up."[62]

It seems funny to me now; he knew me so well that he had to do the hard thing. He didn't give me much of a choice. He said, "Get up," and I felt this tingling power and change rumbling within my body. My bony legs, I thought they might explode. It wasn't like the semi-healing I had seen in those who made it to the pool first; it was terrifyingly exhilarating.

The feeling of my lower body coming to life, growing, my hips becoming liquid, then straight, then strong; I was captivated in the works of the miracle worker in front of me.

I jumped up; I mean, I sprang from the ground into the air and landed on my now-strong legs. All my old friends were gasping; my old lady friends were squealing with joy in a weird sort of reverse grieving.

I was breathing hard, feeling dizzy with disbelief, looking down at my legs, strutting back and forth, and leaping like a baby goat, and then I went to the man who had said, "Get up."

He was crying with joy; he knew.

He loved me; why, I still don't know, but he loved me so much

---

[62] John 5:8.

that he wouldn't allow me to be afraid of life anymore. He couldn't allow me to finish my life not knowing the joy that comes through risk, failure, and worthwhile pain.

He knew.

He would no longer allow me to withhold who he had created me to be: to share life and love with others without fear or withholding. As I stared into his kind, beautiful, and joy-filled eyes, I could see he wanted me to know what he knew.

He wanted me to know the joy of connecting with all the children he had made.

In fact, I now know, yes, I am a father now. I am a husband, against every logical idea of possibility for someone who had wasted nearly forty years of his life. He set me up with the perfect wife, and he set my wife up with the perfect kids. And he set the kids up with the perfect parents.

So Shabella is my beautiful wife. She was a temple prostitute, a Syrian half-breed by birth. She had three beautiful children by unknown fathers. She was getting on in years, and she and her children were living in the shadows of the streets and sometimes outside the walls of the town.

He knew it.

He showed up in her life one day and treated her like she is.

He treated her like a precious and beautiful daughter, not a scarred and evil sinner. It took a few months for her to even start believing him, but she was finally too tired to fight his love. This wasn't another man just needing to lift her skirts to meet a need and move on; he was the real deal. She and her children followed him and wouldn't leave his side.

That was how we met; neither of us could leave him. We started talking, and although we didn't feel worthy of being married, well, he knew.

After sitting in my habitual safety of helplessness, Jesus brought me into the fierce and terrifying real world of pain, risk, joy, love, children, friends, giving, losing, and most of all, Yeshua.

He knew.

And so, now I take my wife and kiddos down to the patio, and we share our stories of hope, pain, risk, love, and impossible healing.

And we ask the people there, "Do you want to be healed?"

We know.

UNPACKING THE LAME MAN AT THE POOL

This story has challenged theologians and serious students of scripture.

Very little is told of the backstory of this injured man; what age was he when he lost his ability to walk? Was it an accident or a disease?

There is none of that information, just a curious question by Jesus: "Do you want to be healed?"

Seems a bit cruel, but sadly, in the reality of life (and those of us in the therapy/counseling side of humanity especially know this), too often people find their worth and esteem in being a victim.

Much good research has been done on what is called the "locus of control," and the findings are highly consistent that those who take responsibility for their positive and tenacious response to the hard and unfair events of life are the most joyful and mentally healthy folks on the planet.

The healthy side of this is someone with an internal locus of control, meaning the healthiest among us perceive their life is up to them. While we cannot choose everything that happens to us, we can choose our response to it. This is more accurately known as a bilocal locus of control because it admits there are just some things in life that are not fair. We don't choose the circumstance; some unfair things just happen in life. A person with a bilocal locus of control chooses to deal with the bad events anyway. Yeshua demonstrates in his walk on earth that we do have the power to choose our response to any circumstance.

The opposite end of the spectrum is the person with an external locus of control: someone who sees their lot in life as the result of bad breaks, oppression, or bad luck.

With all of this in mind, let's make a few applications from this story of healing:

BE VICTORIOUS, NOT A VICTIM

We can settle for being a victim, but Yeshua came to make us victorious.

If you're friends with counselors or therapists, ask them if they ever had a client who was improving greatly, but when they tried to terminate counseling, the client absolutely freaked out. Although they cannot reveal specifics, if they have been doing their job for long, they most certainly have.

It is common for people who have experienced hurt or trauma in their lives to come to see their worth in terms of their trauma, whether it's PTSD, abuse, or something else. They let people know what they went through, and naturally there is sympathy. They go to counseling (as is proper) and begin dealing more fully with the original issue.

This is all good, unless the comfort provided by the sympathy of compassionate people, the one-on-one time with a counselor, or the excuse provided by the hurts of the past becomes their life. It's a gig.

In this fictional interpretation of the man beside the pool, it was just pointed out that the life of the invalid has some advantages. There are particular friends, benefits, and help available to this man.

Further, there may be some absolution. In other words, "I'd like to be a better spouse but I was abused" kind of thinking.

Don't get me wrong; the body keeps score. If there is unresolved hurt in your past, it will eat into who you are until you deal with it. There are scars from abuse, trauma, and true oppression that will hurt when touched, until the day you die.

But guess what? The Messiah has something to tell you:

"Get up."

I've worked with people who've been hurt by a parent or someone else, and they are struggling to find the strength to move past it; the starting statement I use comes from my own experience growing up with a neglectful father:

"How much more of your life do you want to give to your abuser? I have chosen to strive to learn from the experience and move on in who the Christ says I am. I personally do not care to give one more minute to my oppressor."

The big question here is, what does the abundant life your Lord promised you in John 10:10 actually look like? Permanent therapy sessions? A lifetime of excuses why you let others down because someone let you down? People who avoid you because if they ask,

"How are you?" they don't have two hours to listen to your always woe-is-me, permanently negative story?

What does the abundant life provided through Yeshua the Christ look like for someone who was badly hurt?

The promises of grace, mercy, peace, and love are not limited by your trauma. You need to deal with your trauma; just understand that at some point, you must find your peace in who God says you actually are. We must embrace the truth he taught: "No one can serve two masters."[63]

If I imagine sitting in front of Jesus back in those days and hearing him say, "No one can," well, he's got my attention. If I am considering that he is the Messiah (the Anointed One of God) and is teaching me that he and the Father are one, well, when he tells me no one can do something, I want to know what that thing is that no one can do.

Two masters: either he rules our life in increasing peace, love, mercy, and grace, or we serve ourselves by becoming a victim of mere humanity. I am not at all minimizing the struggle of overcoming abuse, trauma, or physical issues; it is natural to struggle with hurts of the past, physical, emotional, or mental.

But our calling in Christ is supernatural.

We must "get up" and take that mat of incapacitation out of the dung gate[64] of Jerusalem and burn it on the trash heap. Doing so requires that we spend serious time sitting, talking, reflecting, and listening to our merciful Savior. Put down your devices and addictive substances, and dwell in your pain with God himself.

---

[63] Matthew 6:24.

[64] The dung gate was a small gate in the walled city of Jerusalem through which the poop and other trash was taken out and dumped.

Further, we need to be with his people so they can help us be who God says we are (and we can help them do the same). This is to be a two-way street; we must share in our goal to be victorious and full of peace in Christ, not a permanent invalid sitting by a pool, making excuses.

> **TAKEAWAY 1:** If you have been sitting comfortably by the pool of victimhood, get up. Learn to become who God himself says you are.

DO NOT ENABLE

If you love someone who is living in their victimhood, be loving, as Jesus was.

I'm a prolific enabler. I have often found my worth (because of traumas of my past) in being the savior, doing everything in my power to make it easier on those who are hurting or weak.

Oh yes, and then I would play the "look at me" card for all my selfless service to those who needed help.

We who enable are also serving two masters. We serve Christ (primarily with our mouth), and we serve ourselves by being a substitute savior to those who need a more proper word. We have found our worth in being a substitute savior to our glory.

The proper word to a person sitting perpetually by the pool of Bethesda requires discernment through prayer (and much listening). We must understand those in our life who are hurting and discover what they need. Have they ever actually looked head-on at the hurtful event and just owned the reality of it? Have they sat down with trusted and spiritually wise friends to work through the pain/anger/confusion and found their peace in Christ and who he knows they are?

If not, encourage them to seek that level of help.

But if you perceive they have done all of that and are resting in a victim identity (instead of a brother or sister to Christ reality), then you need to say a version of what Jesus said in this encounter:

"Get up."

If you have been enabling their victim status, then repent, apologize, and encourage them to be who God knows they are.

He died for us all; we need to live that.

TAKEAWAY 2: If you know people who are lounging by the victim pool, find ways to encourage them to "get up" and be who God says they are. If you have been an enabler, repent and become a truly loving person, instead. Learn to speak up and do what helps a person to be who God died for them to be. Let Yeshua be the Savior.

Chapter Six

I AM ONE OF THEM
The Unknown Pharisee

I LOOKED AROUND THE ROOM; IT WAS A STRANGE SCENE.

The men of the council were all dressed in their robes, their phylacteries very prominent, the impressive headgear, and flowing grey beards. In front of this stately and somber group stood two young men, dressed like laborers.

It didn't seem very fair, but I didn't care.

We had them just where we wanted them.

These two young guys had met their match. They were once again spreading their heresies; they were so bold as to go into the temple, and they drew a crowd.

We gave the order and had them arrested.

Now we watched as the two men stood in front of us.

It was going to be epic. The leaders of our faith and community were all there. The chief priest, his esteemed family, and anyone who was somebody was there.

These were the best and brightest, the most learned, experienced, and powerful men of Jerusalem.

They would eviscerate these two pathetic troublemakers.

Everyone feared the council; just being brought before us would likely end their ridiculous little sect of the late nobody from Nazareth we had finally rid ourselves of. This would be the end of the myths and the heresies this man had taught.

"By what power or by what name did you do this?"[65] thundered the question from the council chief.

Some of men of the council quietly chuckled.

Others smirked or glared at the young fools; word on the street was that they were both fishermen. One of them was not even twenty years old yet.

We knew they would likely fold in front of us. No one wanted to be at odds with us.

I actually felt a little embarrassed; after all, I remembered how fearful and uncertain I was at their age. We wouldn't have to be here long today.

"Rulers of the people and elders, we are being examined today concerning a good deed done to a crippled man."[66]

What? No, that's not why we brought them in. These two heretics were spreading lies, but you know, that guy they healed—

"By what means this man has been healed, let it be known to all of you and to all the people of Israel that by the name of Jesus Christ of Nazareth, whom you crucified."[67]

There was a sudden onrush of grumbling amongst the council. That name, Jesus Christ of Nazareth, just another fool who claimed to be the Messiah; that name roused everyone's anger. Yes, these

---

[65] Acts 4:7.

[66] Acts 4:9.

[67] Acts 4:10.

two must be silenced. We were the experts in the law, we had the sacred scripture, how would these two uneducated fishermen know how to recognize the Messiah?

Crucified this supposed rabbi? What else would we do? Anyone who stands against the truth of God must be—

"Whom God raised from the dead—by him this man is standing before you, well."[68]

For some reason, that statement got my attention. I could hear my fellow council members scoffing and threatening the two fishermen, but my mind was suddenly drawn to Rachel, my sister-in-law. She was a follower of the Nazarene. She had been to my house a few weeks ago; we had eaten together and enjoyed an evening as family. Pua, my wife, had asked me not to talk about her following the Nazarene, and so I didn't. But late in the evening, while my wife and Rachel were cleaning, and I was talking with her husband, I heard a quiet but excited exchange.

"He is alive. I saw him; I touched him," I heard Rachel's hushed voice say. I strained to hear more of the conversation; I was excited yet also disturbed.

No one in the council had believed—well, except for Nicodemus and a few of the others who had left us at about the time that we had the Nazarene killed.

And there was another problem: Rachel and Pua were special girls. Their father, a very wise and respected Pharisee, had trained them up like most families trained their boys. They were smart, good thinkers, and they knew the scripture. I always treasured my conversations with Rachel because she was my intellectual equal;

---

[68] Ibid.

actually, she was more learned than me. She had wisdom, a strength of character, and a sense of clarity I admired and envied.

When she told me of her belief in the Nazarene, I was shocked, but she was not someone I could accuse of being simple or ignorant. Her reasons for belief, well, they often led to an argument, but I could never refute them.

Sure, I would present the arguments against the false rabbi I heard in the council and at the synagogue. We told people the Messiah was not to arise from Nazareth. Anna was an investigator; according to the Nazarene's mother, she had had her baby in Bethlehem, which was, of course, the place the Messiah was to come from.[69]

She even brought up an obscure passage from Isaiah and pleaded with me not to do what the passage stated: that the Messiah's own people would reject him.[70]

She was so convincing, but why couldn't my fellow scholars on the council see it?   I looked again at the two fishermen and the man who had been healed. I had seen this man nearly every day for the past five years (or had it been ten?). His family would bring him to the Beautiful Gate, where he sat on a rug and begged for alms. His legs were nothing but shriveled bone. He was skinny and his face gaunt and hopeless.

I looked at him closely, standing in front of me on muscular legs. This man had been healed.

"This Jesus is the stone that was rejected by you, the builders, which has become the cornerstone," one of the fishermen said

---

[69] Micah 5:2–5.
[70] Isaiah 6:9–10.

clearly. That verse, that psalm[71] was one Rachel had spoken of just last night. She was making another plea to me, to consider everything that had happened up until now was what the scripture had foretold. I felt suddenly hot and looked around at the faces of these men who had long been my friends; could they all be wrong? Was I wrong? How was this man standing here on strong legs? How could these two fishermen—

"There is salvation in no one else, for there is no other name under heaven given among men by which we must be saved."[72]

I braced for the outpour of shouting. I knew the council would explode against these two simple men for saying such.

There was utter silence. I looked at these men again; they all were staring at the healed man, speechless. Each of us had walked past him, what, every day for years? We had seen his useless, flesh-covered bones folded awkwardly beneath him.

Everyone stared at the man and then looked downward and at each other, hoping for a word, any word to respond to the simple fishermen.

"Please, leave us for a moment," the council chief said.

"Please"? That was not like him. The three men left the room, and the curtain in the door was pulled. No one said anything for a few minutes.

Then one old priest said, "These fishermen, they have spent a lot of time with the Nazarene; they learned his ways of trickery to attempt to silence us."

Trickery? They just said the man we all knew had been completely unable to walk was now leaping, running, and standing

---

[71] Psalm 118:22–24.

[72] Acts 4:12

on strong legs in front of us because of Jesus. What kind of trickery was that?

Plus, these two disciples of the Nazarene were strangely calm. We had brought other messianic pretenders before this group before; people were not normally calm before us. Of course, their calmness was very much like the Nazarene's on the night of the trial.

"What shall we do with these men?" the chief asked. "For that a notable sign has been performed through them is evident to all the inhabitants of Jerusalem, and we cannot deny it. But in order that it may not spread further among the people, let us warn them to speak no more to anyone in this name."[73]

"In this name?" What, are we afraid to say Yeshua of Nazareth? I felt my anger rising within me. Yes, a miracle had been performed. Can the enemy of our great God perform healing? Where did these simple men get the power to heal? Where did this calmness originate? Why are we afraid of that name?

I started to speak; I stood, and all of the men looked toward me. I suddenly felt afraid; why can't they see what I am seeing?

"Do you have something to say?" the chief of the council queried respectfully.

"Well, I was thinking." I paused; I would lose everything if I said what was on my heart: my respect, my friends, and perhaps even my livelihood. I mumbled, "I was thinking we should bring the men back in."

I sat down.

Fear; why do I fear these men? If God is God, will he not give me all I need? Had not the great prophets of old also been opposed?

---

[73] Acts 4:16, 17.

I once again thought of Rachel, her courage in sharing her belief that the Nazarene rabbi was the Messiah.

She had seen him, touched him, after the tomb? She was a woman of truth; I knew her well enough to know she would not lie. I wished I had her strength. I wished I had the same calm resolve the two fishermen had. I wished I had the joy of the healed man.

I looked up. The two fishermen had returned and still looked calm; the lame man (well, no longer lame) was holding on to the one known as Peter, and he was smiling and looking occasionally down at his strong legs.

"You are to speak no more in the name of the Nazarene."

The words of the chief were strong and clear.

The two fishermen looked at each other and silently nodded. The lame man, the formerly lame man, had a look of disbelief on his face.

"Whether it is right in the sight of God to listen to you rather than to God, you must judge, for we cannot but speak of what we have seen and heard."[74]

There was a loud gasp and sudden cursing from the council. The lame man laughed; he had a beautiful smile on his face.

"If you speak in his name again, you will be fully punished," yelled the chief.

The three men looked at each other, shrugged their shoulders, and said, "We understand."

After a moment of silence, the chief looked down at his feet and said, "You are free to go."

I watched the healed man walk out, with his arms wrapped

---

[74] Acts 4:19, 20.

around the two fishermen; the absolute joy on his face was like the look of a man with a great secret.

It was like the look on Rachel's face when she told me why she believed in the Nazarene.

I looked back at the stern faces of the men around me; why was I afraid of their disapproval? How could they acknowledge this great miracle, that none of us could even begin to explain, and think of nothing but preserving ourselves as the center of authority and respect?

We had killed the Nazarene. Why? The stories of the kindness, the healing, and Lazarus? We had schemed together to kill Lazarus. I had met him.

I was supposed to set him up; to figure out how we could entrap him and kill him, I went to see him, but he was so kind. He somehow knew why I was there; he embraced me and said I must do what I was sent to do.

He seemed so comfortable with death, and so I asked him, "Are you not afraid of what we will do to you?"

He burst out laughing, then he quickly got serious and put his hand on my shoulder. "My brother, if you would just sit down with Yeshua, you would see. You would know." His tears began to flow. "You would see that to know him is to know peace."

He exuded calm, peace, love: all the things Rachel continually praised the Nazarene for.

All the things, I realized as I sat on the council in that moment, I did not have.

None of us here had what the rabbi from Nazareth had.

I suddenly stood up, and once again, all the men looked at me, expecting something.

I removed my headdress and placed it on my chair.

"I'm sorry, I am no longer going to be one of you."

"Reuben, what do you mean? You are one of—"

"I am," I interrupted, and thinking of the resolve and courage of my sister-in-law, I strongly said, "one of them." I pointed toward the door the three men had just walked through. "I am now a follower of the Nazarene."

I grabbed the neck of my robe and tore it sharply; it ripped down the side seam, almost to the tassels. I slipped it off my shoulders and stepped forward, now wearing only my undergarment.

"Reuben, you cannot. The man was a heretic." The chief was standing, shouting at me.

"No, he is a healer; he is the Messiah."

I walked confidently toward the door, expecting shouting or maybe a rush of feet. I expected fully to be grabbed, taken to the edge of town, and stoned.

I found myself walking alone, yet feeling in good company. I went to Rachel's house and walked inside.

She looked surprised and asked, "What is wrong Reuben?" She was quite shocked to see me only wearing my linen undergarment.

I laughed and replied, "I am of Christ."

She covered her mouth and squealed, "Let me get you one of Asher's robes, and then we will celebrate."

UNPACKING THE UNKNOWN PHARISEE

In the story of Nicodemus in John chapter 3, Nicodemus states, "Rabbi, we know you are a teacher come from God." Nicodemus was not the only person amongst the Jewish religious elite who saw and heard enough of Jesus to know that in spite of the official party line, this rabbi was something special.

In the story of Peter and John before the council, the religious leaders make a stunning admission: "What shall we do with these men? For that a notable sign has been performed through them is evident to all the inhabitants of Jerusalem, and we cannot deny it."[75]

There are a few important lessons we can take away from this remarkable trial:

◼ LOVE GOD WITH ALL YOUR MIND, REALLY

History, from biblical times to the present, clearly shows that people often go along with falsehoods that are contrary to what is clearly true.

Much research has been done on the reasons why the atrocities of the twentieth century occurred, in which more than 200 million people were killed through the actions of their own governments, excluding war casualties.[76]

Many of these massive kill-offs occurred through a process known variously as mass formation, mass delusion, or mass psychosis.

In such situations, an idea is forwarded and promoted by a small group; certain conditions exist that cause the populace to feel isolated and have no control over their lives, no meaning, a generalized nonspecific anxiety, and a strong sense of anger.

Under these conditions, a message put out by the governing

---

[75] Acts 4:16.

[76] Retrieved from https://reason.com/volokh/2022/11/09/data-on-mass-murder-by-government-in-the-20th-century/.

body is believed by about 30 percent of the people; another 40 percent go along with it to avoid conflict, and taking violent action against others results. Atrocities such as the Holocaust and the Russian purges under Stalin and Lenin and others are examples the results.

The big takeaway in the case of the ruling council is this: Whether you are on an expert council or just a regular Joe (or Josephine) in the crowd, you must have the courage to look at the evidence, think for yourself (something few people are trained to do), and then stand for what is right and against that which is evil.

In this example, our fictional Pharisee is encouraged by his honest, intelligent, and truthful relative. One thinking and loving person can change the course of others in their life.

This all sounds good and comforting until you find yourself facing the leadership of your church, community, or family, taking a stand for Christ, truth, or righteousness that no one else will see.

The work of Solomon Asch and others following his experiments do show that people often have trouble standing up for what is obviously true.[77] This challenge of being an odd man out is daunting for many, perhaps even more so in a religious group setting.

I have had preachers, elders, and others in my tradition of faith express confusion as to why certain groups believe what they believe, when the truth seems so obvious.

I point out that most of us do not come to faith by examining all of the evidence ourselves, but rather we are handed a package of beliefs, explained to us by believers, and we simply accept their

---

[77] See article at https://www.simplypsychology.org/asch-conformity.html.

explanation because they sound good to us, and everyone else believes it too.

To avoid this, as was said in an earlier lesson, we must learn to be humble and realize that we generally are not trained to think, nor do we often choose to think.

When someone challenges our cherished beliefs, we should listen and consider asking why this person believes what he or she believes, and further, what is our evidence for believing what we hold to be true?

Given the examples of the trial of Peter and John before the council, as well as the crimes against humanity of the twentieth century, we must avoid being overly locked into thinking we are the most intelligent and enlightened people on the planet; we should show grace to others.

It is terrifying for me to think, given my legalistic background (I would have been a great Pharisee in earlier life), that had I been alive at the time of Christ, I likely would have rejected him. How sad to think of all those men and women who rubbed elbows with the prophesied Messiah, who was doing miracles and speaking truth, yet they could not see him because of their groupthink, the strong but wrong opinions of the religious elite, and the fear of the disapproval of their peers.

Thinking is serious work. Decisions about whether Yeshua of Nazareth was God in the flesh is a huge and controversial topic. "You just have to have faith" is bad and unbiblical advice, given the way this phrase is meant. That kind of faith is wishful thinking.

Yet the follower of Christ is called to this definition of faith:

"Faith is the assurance of things hoped for, the conviction of things not seen."[78]

As other versions of the Bible say, assurance is "substance" or "evidence." Our faith is to be arrived at through the study of the evidence for the truth of who Jesus was and is. Faith is not wishful thinking in spite of the evidence.

Once we have done that, we must remember the challenge of Joshua to Israel as they began the conquest of the Promised Land:

> If it is evil in your sight to serve the LORD, choose this day whom you will serve, whether the gods your fathers served in the region beyond the river, or the gods of the Amorites in whose land you dwell. But as for me and my house, we will serve the LORD.[79]

Here is the primary lesson of this fictional enhancement about Peter and John before the Jewish council:

TAKEAWAY: Do the hard work, in humility, and consider what you believe and why you believe it. Understand that many heresies are passed along through the process of people with good intentions operating out of fear; wrong beliefs are propagated and continued through groupthink, fear, and intimidation. Have the courage to stand for what you have studied and determined to be true, with humility.

---

[78] Hebrews 11:1.

[79] Joshua 24:15.

Chapter Seven

SORRY, BRO
The Unfortunate Raising of Lazarus

UNBELIEVABLE, SIMPLY UNBELIEVABLE.

I cannot find the words for the stunning view here, the joy in my heart, in this new body.

How long had I been here? I had no sense of time anymore; a lifetime, minutes, days?

I remember being sick, a high fever, unreal pain in my gut. Mary and Martha were wiping the sweat from my body and trying to keep me cool but could do nothing for the pain. Martha was first worried, fretting, and then became angry.

It seems funny now, but it wasn't then; I shared her hope and frustration.

"If only Yeshua were here, he would heal you," Martha said. "Where could he be?"

She sent her cousins and a neighbor to find him, but they did not return in time, I surmise.

My pain grew worse, and finally, I wanted to die. Living was just not doable anymore.

Then suddenly, shalom, the most unreal yet incredible experience of my life: death?

I found myself in a different place, in blinding light, but not just light, in a presence of immenseness, of power, of purity, of justice, of glorious and soothing music—of the Father?

I had been changed; I was me, but no more pain. I had a body, but it was perfect, flawless. I was light. I could not find the words to express; there were no words grand enough to even tell myself what I had become or what I had been all along. Was this the real me the whole time I had been alive? No, I was now alive. I was so alive.

But yes, this was the me underneath the me. I was changed but the same, only now, I was in the presence. The light. The glory. The joy.

I found myself prostrate before the presence, terrified. Overwhelmed? Unsure? I wanted to praise what, no, who, I perceived in every way someone could be perceived, but his presence? I could not speak. I felt as though I might die, but I had died.

I was more alive than ever; no, it was as if I was alive for the first time, not just seeing these people around me as I peered from the glorious floor of the throne room. These people, their faces were full of shalom, kindness, joy. I had never realized how the strain of the earth put such a mark on our faces; these faces here in the presence looked more like newborn children, yet fully grown.

But these people to my right and left, as I dared to look briefly, I didn't just see them; I somehow experienced them. I knew them somehow; it was as if—

Suddenly, the most beautiful and astonishing sound, a voice, but like the wind, the rushing Jordan, disturbing yet full of love, full of laughter.

"Yes! Welcome, Lazarus. We've been expecting you. My son speaks of you continually; we have much to share." And he laughed—the Holy One.

I peered up carefully; wow, I felt faint, completely undone. I pushed my face downward, but then a hand, a gentle touch filled my body with something; what was it?

"Do not fear," said the voice, and then that beautiful laughter of love. "You'll get used to this, Laz; you were made for this. We just have to wear the scars of the old earth off of you."

And he continued laughing as he pulled me off the floor. He stood by my side, his arm around me; oh, that moment. How could I continue to exist in that extreme joy? But I suddenly understood something. I was now, forever, who I really had been, all along.

I was lost in musing, completely consumed in thought, but I could feel the Father looking at me. I looked at him, at his eyes, the power and love that flowed through them, unlike any eyes I had seen, yet familiar. He was smiling broadly; he knew, he knew what I was thinking, and somehow, I knew in that moment what he was telling me. He was confirming, yes, I was now what Yeshua had always been trying to tell me I was. I looked away from his beauty and laughed, and then suddenly, the whole room was filled with laughter and music.

It all meshed together: the laughter of thousands of people and angels.

Created spirits—the truest people of all. I was now, no, I was now getting who I was and who everyone else was. This was the real place, which would never change. I had always pictured this as some momentary destination, where I would be changed into something different, but now I was grasping it. I was more me than I had ever realized, but this was the real me I had always been.

I laughed again; the Father squeezed me and laughed with me, and the thousand voices laughed and sang. I was suddenly surrounded.

My mother, father, grandparents, my best friend from childhood who had died too early, oh yeah, there was that guy: Abraham. I somehow knew him. I couldn't wait to talk to him more, this place, in the presence. I was so, so at home.

How long had I been here? There was no time here, no night; I never got tired, yet I rested like I have never rested before. There was just joy and shalom and the presence. I was sitting on a hill now, just taking walks to look over the countryside—the countryside?

This place went on forever; every time I topped a hill, there was stunning beauty. How did he do this? He loves beauty; he loves the beauty of all things he has created, and so today, I sat and marveled at the sight of a new valley, a stunning river with a color of water that, once again, I cannot describe.

"It never gets old; there is always more to see," a gracious and kind voice announced from behind me.

I looked; it was Michael the angel. He sat down beside me, looking down into the same valley. I scanned his face; he was rather glorious looking, smiling as he took in the view.

"I can't believe I'm here, Michael; it's just so ..." My words trailed off; there just were no words to describe how I felt, what I was experiencing.

"We get that pretty much every time someone shows up," he responded, laughing. Then he looked a little more serious, grew inquisitive, and said, "So were you afraid of dying? I mean, I've always been back and forth between here and there; it's a little different for us."

"Oh yes, I feared death a lot. I just couldn't picture it. I guess it was a struggle to think about me not existing, well, you know, back there. I just couldn't picture what came next; death just seemed like a hard end. I never foresaw this. But now that I'm here, wow, it's a thrill, every moment, just knowing there is no more need to fear, no more pain, no more loss."

"Well, about that," Michael interrupted, "we need to talk; we need you to do something."

"Sure, I'm yours, I mean, I'm his." I laughed; my old earth language sounded kind of silly here.

"You're going back."

I could not grasp what he was saying; going back? I could feel my eyes narrowing as he looked at me; he wasn't joking (and there had been some serious joking here in the presence). Did he mean I'm going back—

"The Son, you know, Yeshua, he's calling you back; it's part of the plan." Michael's face, well, it was strange; it was the closest thing to sadness I had seen here. It wasn't like an earth sadness—more like, he understood my struggle.

"I'm going back?"

I sat there for a minute, silent, struggling to grasp what, why, or how this could be? I had no desire to go back; this wasn't supposed to happen, was it?

"Do people often go back?" I asked.

"It's rare. You know, occasionally a prophet or the Son brings someone back; it's just a mercy to someone on earth, usually. A widow needs her son or something like that."

"Why me? I just got here, I think?" I laughed; I really had no idea of how long I had been really alive, or as we call it back there, dead.

Michael laughed. "Listen, the Son needs you. This is part of showing his power, his authority, and his compassionate love. He's going to call you back into the tomb, and from there, well, back there."

I sat stunned. I knew it was right, it was true. I suddenly realized even more than before how vital to the world Yeshua was. I did not want to go, but the others, back there, they needed to know that Yeshua—

"Okay, I'm good; how long do I—" I busted out laughing again, realizing I hadn't totally lost the remains of the earthly me. I guess I would still be able to make it there.

Michael was laughing too, then we both got quiet and just enjoyed the view. It was a good moment.

"So, can I ask," I said softly, "when is he going to be done down there?"

Michael continued looking down at the river and replied, "Above my decision level, my friend; he'll be back when he, well, he'll be back when it is finished."

"When the world is finished?" I queried.

"No, when his ... when he becomes the final perfect lamb." And this time, it was his voice that trailed off. He seemed unable to speak any further about what would happen.

The shades of color in the sky were changing, somewhat like a sunset on earth, or maybe it was the sunset on earth that was like the sky here. The light emanated from the throne; the changes in the hue were just, I was perceiving, a reflection of the varying and amazing beauty of the Father.

This was very good.

"Hey, I'm thankful for you, Laz," Michael said softly. "I really see why you and the Son are such great friends back there."

"So you gotta go, you got work to do?" I asked.

"No, *you* do," Michael stated.

"Lazarus, come forth."

The voice, his voice: it came from all around me. My vision dimmed, then suddenly, I was in darkness.

The stench was awful, I retched. My body had never felt so dry, so sick, and so in pain. I tried to blink my eyes, but they too were dry and sticky. I felt a surge of life coming through my body and a life-giving moisture suddenly pulsing through me.

I was in a tomb and felt the texture of a cloth on my face. My hands were covered, no, my whole body was wrapped. That horrid smell, was it me? I strained my right arm and pulled it up through the cloth and ripped the headcloth off. I retched again; this time, I could taste the bitter bile in my throat. I struggled to swing my legs onto the floor from the stone ledge of the tomb; it was still dark, but a light came from the entrance of the tomb.

I was feeling better by the moment, in the dim light I could see my pale skin growing in color, my muscles healing and gaining strength. I was wrapped in a burial cloth; I wiggled my way up to my feet and kicked a little slack so I could hobble. I worked my way toward the light.

I was back.

It was blinding at first, but certainly not like the light I had just left. My vision was still a bit blurry, and I wiped my eyes with my free hand as I struggled to pull the other one out from the cloth.

Then I saw him as I came out of the tomb; he smiled, looked at the two men next to him, and said, "Unbind him, and let him go."[80] The men came running, and they freed me from my death wrap—or was it my life wrap? I soon felt their embraces, and then I walked over to Yeshua; as I approached, he arched his eyebrows and flashed a wry smile.

We embraced; it was good to be back with him again. As we hugged, he laughed quietly and said, "So sorry, bro. I am so sorry for bringing you back."

We both then pulled away and laughed; we laughed for at least a minute. Suddenly, a minute made sense again. I looked around; everyone was sort of laughing, but they all seemed to realize that Yeshua and I had an inside joke they were missing.

I leaned in close to his face and said, "You tried to tell me before; oh, how you tried to tell me. It was so ... so ..."

"I know, I know, right?" His face was full of joy. We could share the knowledge of the gift he was here to offer everyone. "Hey, my Father told me how you and he are big buddies now. It's a family thing, right?"

"Well, you see," I started, looking around, "I don't want to be here. This is for you, you know?"

His face looked serious, then a bit mischievous.

"Okay," he said quietly, leaning toward me closely, "just so you know, the Pharisees and priests are going to want you dead, so there's that."

---

[80] John 11:44.

"Don't try to cheer me up," I said to my Savior and friend, and once again the laughter came on between us.

"Yes. Oh, how I love you, Yeshua; you are such a stunning blessing. Always seeing the bright side of things."

"Hey, there's a couple of sweet girls here who want to hug you for a while; they're dying to see you."

We laughed again. "Dying to see me? They wish they could have," I responded, and now Jesus burst out in a big laugh and turned me toward Mary and Martha; they were on my neck instantly. It felt good, and I once again had tears running down my cheeks.

Soon I would return.

UNPACKING LAZARUS

Lazarus is a fairly minor character in the Bible; John is the only apostle who mentions him. You can (and should) read his story in your Bible, beginning in John 11, with the details of the death threat against him detailed in the next chapter.

He is the brother of Mary and Martha, and he and his sisters lived in the town of Bethany.

This trio were friends of Jesus, who "loved them."[81]

So when Lazarus fell ill, the sisters wanted Jesus to show up and heal him.

Which is exactly what the friend of Mary, Martha, and Lazarus didn't do. The friends sent by the sister found Jesus and told him about Lazarus's illness—yet Jesus did not go to him. He simply

---

[81] John 11:5.

said, "This illness does not lead to death. It is for the glory of God, so that the Son of God may be glorified through it."[82]

Eventually, Jesus headed toward the city of his friends while telling his companions, "Our friend Lazarus has fallen asleep, but I go to awaken him."[83] This is what makes the story interesting (and this is the basis for this enhanced story).

Jesus knows he is going to bring Lazarus back into his human form, yet when he sees Mary's troubled heart and her tears, he writes what has been the favorite verse of many of us asked to quote a scripture, John 11:35: "Jesus wept."

The challenge is, was Jesus only motivated by the emotion of his friends Mary and Martha in distress, or was there something very sad about what he was about to do?

I do not know.

But thinking through this possibility is the inspiration for this story of the recall of Lazarus from the presence of our Abba Father, what we commonly call heaven. We get glimpses of heaven through such writers as Isaiah (see Isaiah chapter 6) or from the apostle John in the book of Revelation.

John's words were the inspiration for this puny attempt at helping us envision life in the presence of the Father. John continually uses the phrase "the appearance of," or as the old King James version said, "like unto."

One gets the strong impression that John just could not find adequate words to describe what he was seeing in his experience, but whatever the case, it was glorious beyond describing.

And so, on this earth, we often fear death, but should we at least

---

[82] John 11:4.
[83] John 11:11.

read Isaiah and John, and try to imagine the joys of the presence of the Father?

We can also look at the way people responded when they experienced any small degree of the glory, that is the absolute emanating power, love, grace, justice, purity, and everything else that God is, if they happened to experience it? The normal response was to fall flat on the ground and breathe dust.

With that in mind, my apologies to all for this chapter, as it represents the greatest stretch into biblical historical fiction in this book. How does someone describe what John in the book of Revelation finds to be nearly impossible?

My aim is to help us all see death as a victorious entry into something so inexplicably wonderful that we would be offended at the idea of Jesus bringing us back, as he did Lazarus.

Thus, I do picture this moment as portrayed in the fictional story, where our Lord quietly says to Lazarus, "Sorry, bro."

Here are a few lessons for us:

DO NOT FEAR

Living in fear invalidates Yeshua's intent for you.

Life in a mortal body is dicey. It is dangerous to get out bed in the morning; it is dangerous not to. The people you love and hug in the morning may be dead by the end of the day. You are one missed heartbeat away from eternity, every moment of every day. You can have heart attack, a stroke, or a car accident; break your neck on a trampoline; be shot; contract a fatal disease; or just die of old age.

It is totally natural to fear the loss of your physical life and the pain that goes with it.

Jesus made abundantly clear one of the reasons he agreed to descend to earth:

> The thief [Satan, the deceiver] comes only to steal, kill, and destroy. I came that they may have life and have it abundantly.[84]

A failure to live confidently and joyfully because of the fear of what might happen today robs us of what is true about today because of Jesus. He came to allow us to experience abundance in each day.

Not in the prosperity Gospel mode of abundance, but in the sense that he lived in abundance.

In a world where more and more people feel their lives have no purpose, where too many are isolated and lonely, where they feel powerless and angry, the new covenant mission Jesus died to establish defeats all of these sad conditions.

The reality is, the abundant life on earth can only be found by truly abiding in him. His mission, his intent in his church, is that each of us has a powerful purpose in every moment of every day. Each brother or sister of the Nazarene has the power that flows from the throne through the Spirit of God. Each of us, if we are living true to the heart of the Christ, is a member of a vibrant, loving community of his people (the church), and because of his great love, his revelation to us of our true nature as spiritual creatures with temporary tents called a body, we have no anger or fear.

The best thing that can happen to us is what happened to

---

[84] John 10:10.

Lazarus—death. As the apostle Paul put it so beautifully (and he was nearly put to death so many times):

> So we are always of good courage. We know that
> while we are at home in the body we are away from
> the Lord, for we walk by faith, not by sight. Yes, we
> are of good courage, and we would rather be away
> from the body and at home with the Lord.[85]

The idea that Jesus would have apologized to Lazarus is nothing original; students of the Bible have long suspected the primary reason Jesus wept was because he knew bringing back his friend from the presence of God would be such a deprivation for Lazarus.

Jesus knew this better than anyone on earth.

The question is, do you believe that Jesus's intention for you is abundance—abundance in purpose, connection, impact, and purposeful suffering?

Is your vision of the glory of God anywhere near the magnitude and awesomeness that it should be, so that death seems exciting? It's a hard truth to grasp walking around in a skin-sack. This life is so engrossing, so present, and it seems so real.

But what is more real, what is eternally enduring is the spirit that is you, that for a short period of time resides in a body of flesh, a body that from birth is in the process of dying.

Death and decay is the destiny of your fleshly casing.

Life eternal and glorious is who you actually are right now.

Embrace this; ask our Father to help you know this, and while you are at it, if your courage is sufficient; ask the Father of glory to

---

[85] 2 Corinthians 5:6–8.

show you just as much glory as he knows you can survive. It will transform your fear into raw courage.

Like Lazarus, you will—having experienced the glory of the presence—welcome and even look forward to death.

> **TAKEAWAY 1:** Ask God to show you his glory, meditate in the word, and prayerfully endeavor to begin sensing the reality of life, that you and everyone you see is a spiritual being encased in a temporary fleshly temple. Begin stepping out in courage with the Spirit to experience the abundant life our Savior saved you to experience. The Christ came to give you a life abundant in purpose, his power, life-giving connections (his church), and peace.

CHOOSE FREEDOM

Fear is slavery. You were not redeemed to be a slave of fear.

Warning: This is not an opinion.

> Since therefore the children share in flesh and blood, he himself likewise partook of the same things, that through death he might destroy the one who has the power of death, that is, the devil, and deliver all those who through the fear of death were subject to lifelong slavery.[86]

---

[86] Hebrews 24:14, 15.

Lifelong slavery? That's awful. Why would we choose to be slaves for our entire lives?

But we do.

We fear men, disapproval, conflict, disease, flying, and any number of other things because they may lead to death, pain, or embarrassment.

Here's an exercise I give to people who are struggling in their faith and with fear:

Use your God-given imagination to go to the place where Jesus is being crucified. Sit down on the dirt at the foot of the cross where the Messiah is hanging, writhing in pain. See the caked-on blood, the fresh blood still flowing. Observe the wickedly long thorns from the crown jammed down onto his head by soldiers. Reach out and let a drop of his blood fall onto your palm, and look upon his face.

Then look up to his Father and say, "You know, that's pretty good, but it's not enough for me to believe that you would do anything to calm my fears. I choose fear."

It makes no sense.

But too many of us are fearful simply because we do not sit down for extended and regular periods of time with our Father, with Jesus, with the Spirit, in the Word, engaged in a deep conversation and reflection on what our loving triune God is sharing with us.

Instead, we wake in our beds and pull our phones over our heads and start scrolling. This starts little hits of the brain chemical dopamine flowing, which we keep going all day as we touch, swipe, and bow in worship to these devices (including smart watches, tablets, and laptops).

We go on to continue the stimulation of dopamine through

sugary food, alcohol, video games, vaping, tattooing, cutting, porn, and more.

We rarely sit in silence as spiritual beings, communing undistracted with our spiritual family. We miss out on the liberty our Messiah provides through his victorious death and resurrection.

Where do you choose to go from here?

Continued slavery or glorious courage?

TAKEAWAY 2: It is your choice to embrace slavery or courage. The peace that surpasses understanding must be sought through regular spiritual communion and conversation with God in his Word and through the Spirit. Your call.

Chapter Eight

RISKING IT ALL ON THE RABBI

Jairus and His Daughter

"JAIRUS, SHE IS WEAKER TODAY; SHE MAY NOT MAKE IT."

Bina's voice was quiet but urgent; tears were streaming down her face. I looked around the doorway at the bed where my little Chaya lay. Her face was very pale today; when I had picked her up after Bina bathed her, she was all ribs. She seemed to weigh less than when she was six; now she was twelve years old.

Chaya was our jewel, a special gift from our Lord later in life. Bina had been unable to have children in the right time, but when all hope was lost, my Bina suddenly was feeling sick, and her belly began to grow. What a great gift; the jokes about old Sarai[87] getting pregnant were thrown around us, much to our joy. We enjoyed the joking more than those who teased us. Such joy from our Lord.

---

[87] Sarai was the name of Abram's wife before she had a child in her nineties and became Sarah.

How could the same God who gave us such joy take her away so soon? This wasn't fair; it wasn't what I ever thought God would do.

"What are we going to do, dear? You must do something."

Bina stared at me; flashes of anger, pain, and disappointment flowed from her eyes to mine. My broken heart was racing; I felt helpless.

"I am not the Lord, woman," I snapped angrily. "I cannot heal her, and the doctors have been useless in helping her. What do you want from me?" I walked quickly out of the house.

The sun was oppressive. I was still in my priestly robe, and everyone knew me.

"Hello, Rabbi," a couple said, but then they looked shocked. I realized that my face was a sight, my anger and confusion showed, and my eyes were, well, I was crying.

I quickly turned back toward the house, and there was my Bina, arms outstretched; we landed on each other.

"I'm so sorry, so sorry," she said.

I gently pushed her back into the house and held her close. Why was I so embarrassed to have people see me upset? Angry? Hurting? Did the Torah say a priest was not to show emotion? Not to question the goodness of God? Was this not okay before our Lord? Could I not be just like anyone else—whose daughter is dying?

Oh, Chaya; I held on to my Bina, and we went to Chaya. I put my hand on her beautiful face, that face that had laughed with me, kissed me, and snuggled so close to me, her abba, at the end of every hard day. To her, I was always wonderful, always accepted, and all my problems melted away when we played together.

Her pretty face was hot, very hot. She weakly opened her eyes and smiled. "Oh, Abba ..." Her voice, it was so sweet, but nearly gone.

"Jairus, I'm sorry. I know you have done everything you can. God will know what to do."

"No, dear; I have one thing; there is one."

"You mean ... him?" Bina now looked at me straight on, questioningly.

I suddenly saw the tiredness in her beautiful face; she had aged much the last few months. I had let her down, all because—

"Yes, the Nazarene ..." My voice trailed off.

"But Rabbi Chanoch, he warned us all."

"I have failed to love; I am going to find him. He is our last hope."

"Jairus," Bina's voice called as I turned to leave, and I stopped to hear her kind words. "Shalom, my love, and thank you." She began sobbing as I left the house.

I began walking toward the center of town. I had to find him.

Yes, Rabbi Chanoch had been very direct; this Yeshua of Nazareth was by no means the Messiah, as many thought. He was a fraud, a heretic, and an agent of Satan. The simple people might be fooled by this man, but no synagogue ruler would be.

I got the message; so did my Bina.

To have anything to do with the controversial rabbi would result in losing my position; it had been hard won too. It was who I was.

Amongst the faces in front of me, I saw Kuni, the scribe. I went to him.

"Kuni, I need your help; have you seen the rabbi Yeshua?"

The smile left his face; he was confused. "Are you serious? What do you want with him?"

"I need to talk to him," I said tersely. "It is very important."

"Well, I heard a wild story about him casting out some demons over in the Gerasenes—and it was from a guy who follows him around, so I suppose he may be back in town."

"Where did you see his follower?" I replied.

"Down at the docks," Kuni replied. "I was buying some fish."

"Thank you," I said as I turned and walked quickly toward the docks.

"How is Chaya?" he shouted behind me.

"She's dying," I replied and then stopped, lost in thought.

"You shouldn't be seen with the Nazarene wearing your robe," Kuni called; he had always been a good friend. He knew me well, and he loved me. But I love Chaya.

He was right. This robe made a statement; it would be best for all concerned if I ran back home and put on something that didn't identify me quite so well.

But I had waited too long already. And why?

"Rabbi, how is little Chaya today?"

It was Meir, a member of my synagogue. He was a boat builder and sailmaker.

And, I suspected, a follower of the rabbi from Nazareth.

"Meir," I nearly shouted, "where is your, I mean, the rabbi Yeshua?"

Meir laughed and, a little apologetic, said, "Yes, Jairus, he is my rabbi, that's okay. He is down near the dock, just a couple of streets down from my shop."

I grabbed his right hand with both of mine. "Thank you. Thank you," and I began running.

Why had I waited? Bina and I had talked about him, but I had not told her the whole story; I had been to see Yeshua before.

It was an accident the first time; I was travelling and just happened to see a large crowd and went to see what was happening. There was a lot of excitement and a little grumbling.

There were a few of my type there, standing at a distance, all of us wearing our beautiful robes and watching this man in common clothes with people all around him.

He was healing people.

It was hard to see, and the other priest, rabbis, scribes, and Pharisees were too far off, so I eased in closer. I tried to walk casually, like I was just looking to see who was in the crowd, but I really wanted to hear him. What was he saying that drew people in?

I couldn't believe what I was seeing at first: people with withered legs suddenly jumping and leaping. Little kids who couldn't see, squealing with joy as they suddenly saw their family for the first time.

This had to be fake. This was all arranged.

So I went after a few of the healed people, and I asked some pretty awkward questions. They were clearly offended and insisted they knew nothing of this guy—just heard some rumors about a healer and came. And their family members were healed.

They swore they did not know him; some still didn't even know his name.

I noticed after a while that the healer had gone to a small hill and sat down, and he began to teach. I moved to the edge of the crowd, trying to appear disinterested, but his teaching, it was so unlike anything I had ever heard. I was entranced, and at one point, he was looking straight at me, then he said, "Beware of practicing your righteousness before other people in order to be seen by them."

That was when I left. Something about that really resonated and stung a bit. I went on my way, not entirely sure that this man was a fraud. I should have nothing to do with this false Messiah; it would be costly.

But his words, now, why had I resisted going to see him when Chaya first got sick? Why had I been afraid of letting Bina know I had listened to the rabbi and had seen him heal?

I had to hurry; Chaya was so sick now. What if she dies? I don't know that I might not lose Bina too. Our little girl was our special gift from God; Bina the barren was now "little Sarai" to those who loved her.

Why had I waited?

The docks were ahead; there was no one there. My heart sank. Why had I waited? I looked down the street along the water and saw a few people heading down a side street, and a bit of dust rising over the low buildings; maybe it is him? There always seemed to a crowd around this rabbi.

Why had I waited? The fear of man, as he had warned me?

I pulled up my robe and ran; I had no dignity left. A few fishermen looked at me, pointed, and laughed. I didn't care; my Chaya needed, no, I needed the rabbi. I went around the corner, and there was a large crowd of people. I began pushing people aside, trying to get to the front of the group; I had to find the rabbi. I suddenly saw two robed men, two of my Pharisee friends. I felt a momentary discomfort, but then, no, I must find the Nazarene.

Suddenly, he was there.. I ran to his left side, with my robe still raised, and swung quickly around and fell to his feet. My bare knees ground into the dirt and rocks. I grimaced in pain. I grabbed his hands with mine and begged, "My little daughter is at the point of death. Come and lay your hands on her, so that she may be made well and live."[88]

I felt no embarrassment; this man was my only hope. Forget about the synagogue; I'll tear this robe off my body, just heal my daughter. I stayed at his feet, looking down now, feeling unworthy to look into his eyes. Yes, I had been fearful, practicing my righteousness to earn the approval of my peers. I was still holding his hands, breathing hard from all of my running to find him, my face looking at my now dirty robes and sandals. I was completely terrified of losing my daughter.

I slowly looked up. He was looking at me, and he smiled and nodded. He recognized me?

Then he said, "Take me to her."

I gasped for joy and jumped up; still holding his right hand, I began dragging him through the crowd. I could hear people murmuring. I made brief eye contact with my Pharisee buddies; they looked stern, but I did not care. I nodded at them. They turned away.

The rabbi was coming to heal my Chaya. Nothing else mattered. I was growing tired of the constraints of this robe, anyway.

I was walking at a very fast pace, still breathing hard. I tried not to be impatient with the people in front of me or with the pace of the rabbi. This crisis was all my doing; why hadn't I come sooner?

Suddenly, he stopped, and his hand slipped from mine.

He stopped?

---

[88] Mark 5:23.

I turned around, and he was scanning the crowd behind him. "Who was it that touched me?"[89]

We were all confused; who touched him? Who cares? There were so many people crowded all around him.

"Someone touched me, for I perceive that the power has gone out from me," he told us all.

I was now in a total panic; I needed to get him to move on, but I was at his mercy. I was the one killing my daughter. My foolish pride, my fear of man; this was too much. I didn't deserve to have this good rabbi help me. I stood still, and then I saw her.

A woman came from out of the crowd, smiling, crying, afraid; she was a mess. She fell at his feet.

"My Lord, forgive me, but I have been bleeding uncontrollably for twelve years, and I knew that if I could just touch your clothes, I would be healed. And I am now well."

She was from my synagogue; we had often prayed together for God to help her. She had been to see many doctors. None of us could help.

Twelve years—this poor woman had been suffering for as long as my sweet girl had been alive. I noticed now, her once-pale skin was now vibrant and flushed with color. Her tired eyes now, I could see the joy in her eyes. She looked, well, like a little girl in that moment, and I suddenly realized that everything was going to be okay. This rabbi was the real thing; he was the power of the great God of heaven.

"Daughter, your faith has made you well; go in peace," he said, as he placed his hand upon her head scarf. It was such a beautiful

---

[89] Luke 8:45.

moment, so loving, and he took the time to call her a daughter, to let her know he knew her, that he loved her.

The rabbi looked at me and motioned me on down the road, and I turned and saw our house servant, Rafael. My heart sank; how had he found me, unless Bina sent him? His face was grim, and he walked up to me and bowed.

"Your daughter … is dead. Do not trouble the rabbi anymore."[90]

Dead? Chaya?

Why had I waited? I was suddenly numb; what a foolish, prideful, and worthless father I was. I reached to my collar to tear my robe, when a hand grabbed mine. It was the rabbi. His kind eyes locked onto mine.

"Do not fear; only believe, and she will be well."

I was so lost, so numb, but as we looked at each other, through the sound of his voice, I heard myself say, only within my own head, "Okay; okay."

He smiled, took my hand, and began dragging me down the street toward my house. He knew the way?

Yes, he knew the way; good thing. I'm not sure I could have found it. I felt a bit faint, but calm. There was something in his touch, his confidence, that comforted me.

We were suddenly in the house; the mourners were there, some of my robed friends, and I heard Jesus say over the noise, "Do not weep, for she is not dead but sleeping."

My robed friends laughed, ridiculing the rabbi's pronouncement. But Bina looked at him, stood up, and grabbed his other hand and led him to Chaya's side.

Chaya's face was now colorless. Her mouth hung open; my

---

[90] Luke 8:49.

heart was pounding. I had never experienced this kind of pain. Why couldn't I have been the one to die? I deserved this, the coward that I am.

Yeshua looked at my little girl; he gently cupped her small, pale face, stared at her, and smiled.

It was like he knew her too.

He took her tiny hand in his other hand and said gently, "Child, arise."

She took a quick breath and opened her eyes, and color flushed into her face.

She looked at the rabbi, blinked, and then busted out laughing, "Rabboni!"

She jumped up and hugged him. "He told me I would see—" but suddenly, Jesus put a finger across her pretty little lips, and she quieted with a sweet giggle.

"I know, child. Now give your abba a big hug, he needs one," and Chaya flung herself into my arms with a wild hug. She squeezed me tightly and filled my face with kisses.

She suddenly pulled back and put both of her hands on my face, holding my beard. "Oh, Abba, I knew you would find my Rabboni! He's the—" and she suddenly looked at the rabbi; he smiled and shook his head no, and then they both giggled.

How did she … who told her?

No matter. Bina and I now had our gift back.

We had another gift too, one that our little one had been told about while she was gone.

In spite of Yeshua shushing her, I realized what she was going to say about the rabbi.

Messiah.

UNPACKING JAIRUS

There is much to be learned from this story, and we do have to cut through the fictional elements to discern them.

For Jairus or anyone in his position, there was potentially a very high social cost to following Jesus. We can at the very least deduce that somehow Jairus had heard about or maybe encountered the Nazarene and was at least entertaining the possibility of going to him for help. But it was perceived by him to be risky.

Much as it is today, it is at least perceived to be a risk to follow this Jesus of an old myth-like story. Let's look a couple of things we can learn from Jairus choosing to ask for help from the rabbi from Nazareth:

KNOW, TRUST, AND OBEY

Peer pressure does not stop simply because we get older; it sometimes gets worse.

We adults often lament the peer pressure faced by the children and teenagers of our lives, but let's not kid ourselves. It continues until … well, we die.

There is enormous pressure in the various groups we identify with to conform to accepted beliefs. For Jairus, it seems that most of the religious Jewish leadership had determined that Jesus was a fraud; doing anything other than opposing him was an act of betrayal to true faith in God.

There was enormous pressure from influential, well-meaning, and scripturally knowledgeable people (so-called "experts") to resist this upstart rabbi from Nazareth.

It nearly cost Jairus his daughter's life, and this was unnecessary.

We see throughout the Bible that our Lord often uses a personal crisis to break us out of this peer-induced hesitancy to change our path and seek help from our most capable source: God himself.

Perhaps the greatest takeaway from the story of Jairus, and one that could save us so much trouble, is to learn to sit quietly with God in his Word, to converse and listen reflectively, and to learn to obediently change our behaviors when the Spirit shows the need.

Simple obedience?

Generally, in Western culture, we do not like (at all) the term *submission*.

I was a prime example of this nonsubmissive attitude earlier in life (and still am at times to this day). I always felt I knew better; my friends would often back me in my false knowledge of what was better than what God clearly said, and so I would resist what the Bible revealed as what is true and right, to the point where my ignorant obstinance created a severe crisis for me.

And then, I would realize, had I trusted God and stood in his truth (which requires that I know his truth to begin with), I would have avoided a whole bunch of suffering and harm; I would have been totally blessed by just ignoring my prideful false knowledge, ignoring what everyone around me knew, and just simply obeyed what scripture revealed.

Take a hot tip from Jairus; the big lesson is:

TAKEAWAY 1: Learn to simply obey God without regarding the folk wisdom (false knowledge) of those around you. Just trust and obey.

CHOOSE THE GREATEST TREASURE, EXPENSIVE BUT COSTLY

Simply seeking and obeying Jesus (walking with him) can be very costly in terms of our life in the flesh. It's worth whatever it costs you.

This is the whole point of one of Jesus's parables, and one of the shortest:

> The Kingdom of heaven is like a treasure hidden in a field, which a man found and covered up. This in his joy, he goes and sells all that he has and buys that field.[91]

Jesus, being God, has the ability to say something profound in a very few words.

In this Kingdom story, think of the implications for this man who found a treasure in a field; he sells everything to get the field.

Would not those around him think he was being irresponsible? If they do not know about the treasure (and this is the point of the parable), they would think him reckless? They do not see the value, just as the other religious leaders could not comprehend the value of who the Nazarene was.

Jairus was forced by desperation (the potential loss of a daughter) to risk giving up all he had worked for (his status and livelihood as a synagogue ruler) in order to save the daughter he loved. It likely (although the Bible doesn't tell us) cost him his position. He gained his daughter, and the Messiah, in the process.

---

[91] Matthew 13:44.

Just know, following Jesus at some point will involve a social risk and will possibly look terribly expensive.

He is worth it.

TAKEAWAY 2: Truly following Christ at some point will be expensive. The inspired Word tells us it is worth everything; pay the price.

Chapter Nine

LEARNING WHAT IS REALLY REAL

Thomas the Apostle

"LET NOT YOUR HEARTS BE TROUBLED."[92]

I can still hear his voice; I can see that gleam of light in his eye, that slight laughing look on his face as he said that. I'm pretty sure he especially meant that for me. Things were tense that night for him, but for way too long, things had been tense with me.

My tenseness seemed to be a source of endless amusement for Yeshua.

There was the big one, one of the times I thought he might collapse from laughter. Things were heating up between Yeshua and the religious leaders. Then he told us Lazarus had fallen asleep and we needed to head to Bethany to be with Mary and Martha, but we were all anxious, especially me. We had gotten word that the Jewish leaders were seeking to have Jesus stoned and told him so. He just said something about "light" and it being either in us or

---

[92] John 14:1.

not.[93] I didn't get it; nothing unusual, nor did any of us get the hint about Lazarus being asleep.

So he had to get completely literal, like you would with a small child.

"Lazarus *has* died, and for your sake I am glad that I was not there, so that you may believe. But let us go to him."[94]

I pretty sure I was the small child he was talking to. I wasn't getting any of this.

If Lazarus was dead, how could we go to him? He's dead, right? The religious leaders in Bethany knew that Jesus was good friends not only with Lazarus but with his sisters Mary and Martha too; wouldn't they be expecting him to show up for the grieving?

It just seemed like we were going to Bethany for no good reason, so I spoke from my childish confusion, saying, "Let us go also, that we may die with him."[95]

I didn't see it coming, but the next thing I knew, Messiah was laughing his beautiful laugh.

I was sort of embarrassed, but there was something so unrestrained in him when he laughed. His laugh was special; it was the laugh of someone who knew something I didn't know at the time.

I had been so afraid of death, and my Yeshua had so gently tried to teach me, and all of us learners, to not be anxious about anything. When he sent us out on our first missions without him, his words

---

[93] These words are found in John 11:9, 10.
[94] Ibid., 11:15.
[95] John 11:16.

really struck a nerve: "Do not fear him who can kill the body but cannot kill the soul."[96]

I remember struggling through what he was asking me to think. Not to worry about being beaten, stoned, and possibly killed? The thought confused me; I sat and listened to him, surrounded by the others. I tried to appear confident, but the thought of dying terrified me. I was just Thomas, the twin. Or Judas, if you please, but we had two other Judases in our group, so I became the twin.

The thought, as it seemed at the time, of losing my life—I just couldn't fathom the terror of it. Why would this man, who I and so many others thought to be the promised Messiah, ask me to walk straight into my own death? What good would that do? And I wasn't to be anxious about it?

At the time, I thought I was the only one who struggled with his words (and with him).

I now understand, none of us really got who he was or what he was saying.

So on that night shortly before his death, when he said, "Let not your hearts be anxious," that was one of the darkest nights of my life.

He went on; he said so much more I wanted to believe but could not grasp. I was so literal. And it's not that what he said wasn't literally true; it is just that I was thinking in terms of what seemed most real to me—my own flesh.

His words appealed to me so much: "In my Father's house are many rooms. … I go to prepare a place for you. I will come again

---

[96] Matthew 10:28.

and will take you to myself, that where I am you may be also."[97] That's where I wanted to be, with him. I felt so safe around him, well, most of the time. Except that he would walk into situations that seemed so deadly.

But that night, before he said all of this, he had told us he was leaving and "where I am going you cannot come."[98]

I remember looking at the others; there was near panic, tears—puffy and red eyes. Mary Magdalene whispered to me, "He is all I have; what can we do if we can't follow him?" I felt the same way. I had given up my place in the family business; I thought my future was with him. Why was he going to leave us, and following was what he told us to do from the beginning?

His first words directly to me were, "Follow me."[99] I decided I would, but now the words of his that I could not follow him—I couldn't get it.

And I shared the fear of all the others; what would I do if he left? Without us?

The other Judas, and not the bad one, asked the question that got an answer which really got me thinking. Messiah had said, "Yet a little while and the world will see me no more, but you will see me."[100]

Actually, Peter, James, and John had seen something I hadn't; it changed them, and they began trying to explain what "living in the spirit" meant. It wasn't until after Jesus died that they told us the story of what happened.

---

[97] John 14:2, 3.

[98] John 13:33.

[99] Matthew 8:22 is just one example of this common invitation of the Christ to his disciples.

[100] John 14:19.

Yeshua had invited them up on a mountain, and suddenly, his appearance was completely changed. They said his clothes, his face, and his entire body became purely white, and light was coming from him. It was like power, almost like the sun or a star; energy poured out of him beautifully, power that appeared like a blinding light. Totally amazing, but it got even stranger.

Other people appeared; they soon realized it was Moses and the great prophet Elijah. They also had this shining appearance, and the three were talking with each other.

John especially took from this that we are more than we appear. We are in our bodies, but we are not our bodies. When John and the other two saw Jesus in this state of light, they were seeing the spiritual reality, and that was also who we were, or what we were like, once we shed our bodies.

It was so hard to wrap my head around this. But this was what Yeshua had meant when he said we would see him while the world would not. We would be perceiving the presence of the Lord, but not so much with our eyes or hands, as we did when he was walking with us (or should I say, we were walking with him?).

On that same night, when he said he was going and we couldn't follow, but that we would "know the *way* to where he was going,"[101] I was completely honest in my not even beginning to comprehend what he saying. I asked, "Lord, we do not know where you are going. How can we know the way?"[102]

His answer? It was, "I *am the way*, the truth, and the life. No one comes to the Father except through me."[103] He was the way.

---

[101] John 14:4.

[102] John 14:5.

[103] John 14:6.

It was just so hard to break out of my literal and very fleshly thinking. My body, the things I could touch and see—they just seemed like all there was. It took a lot of time talking with the other believers, and sitting quietly and paying attention to the quiet voices, thinking of the rabbi's teaching, and sensing the presence of my Lord to grow past this limited view.

It was a slow process for me; John and James caught on a lot quicker, but I think seeing Jesus as he most truly was made a huge difference for them. I wish I could have seen what they saw, but in the time since Yeshua ascended, well, I've seen a lot.

The funny thing is, while the Messiah was still with us in the body, he taught us what we needed to hear, but he was patient with us. He knew we couldn't grasp the truth instantly.

Like the one day, when he kept saying the same word over and over again. He was telling us that he was the "true vine"[104] and that his Father was the vineyard owner and caretaker. His Father was in the business of cutting off unfruitful vines, but he would "prune" those that did bear.

Boy, did he ever, and that word Jesus kept using, it annoyed me a bit. It went something like this: "You are clean because of what I have spoken to you. *Abide* in me, and I in you. As the branch cannot bear fruit by itself, neither can you, unless you *abide* in me. I am the vine, you are the branches. Whoever *abides* in me and I in him, he it is that bears much fruit, for apart from me you can do nothing."

He kept on, telling us to abide in him, and he would abide in us; I was getting a bit aggravated, like, "Okay, I get it."

But then, did I? This was right after he said he was leaving

---

[104] John 15:1–17.

and we couldn't follow, that we would be seeing him but the world wouldn't; how in the world am I to abide in that?

It was the spirit thing, or should I say the Spirit? It was such a hard process to slow down my anxious mind (yeah, he told me not to be anxious too) and listen for him, listen for the impressions, to perceive the wind-like movement of our great God through my spirit.

There were so many times in learning to walk in this abiding way that I somehow pronounced the Lord's (or the Spirit's) blessings on my own dubious ideas, but then, he/they would be there, getting my attention, and calling me (gently) to turn around, quiet myself, and listen.

And then, obey. To walk with courage (not my best thing) into dangerous situations, just like he did when he was on earth as a man.

There were a few times I turned away, always heartbroken when I did that, but then the Holy Spirit would comfort me and help me to stand in grace and power once again.

I took more baby steps, sometimes trembling as I went to a person he sent me to. I remembered the time I confronted a priest; he was making some pretty bold threats to, well, in a spiritual sort of way, harm or kill me. He was trying to get me to back down; I had backed down too many times, and my Lord had never let me down. I stood my ground.

The priest never did a thing to me.

But we began pretty quickly to see losses. Peter and John were beaten pretty regularly, and eventually, some of us were killed.

It made for some dark nights, but in the quiet moments of doubt, where I asked myself if I really believed that this worker from Nazareth was really the Messiah, there was only one answer possible.

Absolutely.

I had seen him do things no man can do. He had a knowledge that a mere human could not have had. He had touched me, made me bold, knew my heart, and loved me.

I had even been there on that day when he said, "You will receive power when the Holy Spirit has come upon you, and you will be my witnesses in Jerusalem and in all Judea and Samaria, and to the end of the earth."[105]

It was then, and of course I could never unsee this, that he smiled at me, the one who was so literal, afraid, and tended to doubt everything until I had touched it; he simply left the ground and went upward and disappeared in a cloud.

We all talked about it later; most of us somehow perceived we were in a dream. I felt the world spinning (or was it my head?) as he went upward. My mouth was hanging open, and I remember pinching my forearm with my fingers; it was all so unnatural. But once I felt my own skin, I just raised my arms towards heaven and watched him go.

We were quite the sight, I suppose; suddenly, we heard awesome voices like the wind saying, "Men of Galilee, why do you stand looking up into heaven? This Jesus, who was taken up from you into heaven, will come in the same manner as you saw him go into heaven."[106]

We looked toward the voices; there were two men, gleaming, I suppose in the same manner as Peter, James, and John had seen

---

[105] Acts 1:8, 9.

[106] Acts 1:11.

with Jesus, Elijah, and Moses. I remember feeling shocked but then laughing; I felt more joy than I had ever felt in all of my life.

Yes, Yeshua of Nazareth was the Messiah. The man-God who just flew up into the sky, who had suddenly shown up in my life just three years ago and picked me, the weak doubter, and helped me to learn there is a side of life that is enduring, spiritual, beautiful, and eternal.

The spiritual side of reality is the ultimate reality. It isn't easy to perceive, but it is worth the struggle. The spiritual side of us endures; the physical does not.

Yes, he abides in me, and I abide in him. Yes, his Father has pruned me; I have been beaten, stoned, spat on, threatened, and excluded. I have lost friends, I've been called a "Samaritan" and a dog, and I have had some dark nights where I couldn't see any hope.

But the reality is, he abides in me, and I in him. The Holy Spirit guides me each day. Every day is a day to walk with Yeshua; the friend that I see who most of the world cannot. I wake up each morning knowing and expecting I will walk with him and he will show me where to join him in his work.

Every day is the Lord's day.

I am abiding in him, he abides in me.

If I live, he abides and lives in me.

If I die, I shall see him in his greatest glory, and I can't wait.

And they wonder why I smile.

UNPACKING THOMAS

I grew up knowing him as "doubting Thomas," as if he were the only doubter amongst the apostles, or that we are much different than he was.

Let's face it, all of the disciples struggled to grasp the reality of the spiritual. All of them struggled with fear. Have you noticed how common the message of not fearing is with the Lord?

With that in mind, let us take a couple of life lessons from Thomas:

SPEND SUBSTANTIAL TIME
ALONE WITH JESUS

If those who walked side by side with Jesus in the flesh had trouble understanding him, will we not also struggle?

In my faith tradition, there was a common claim that the message of the Christ was "simple," and no one should have any trouble understanding it.

What a load of garbage.

Jesus was, is, and always will be a challenge for us, and thus eternity is not too long of a time to sit with him and grow in our knowledge. His message of who he is, who we are, salvation, justification, and propitiation are not simple things for any generation to grasp.

These things are foreign and supernatural to our everyday experience on earth, unless we learn to perceive them.

There is an amazing scene in the Old Testament, after Moses made new tablets to replace the ones that were destroyed when Israel was found to be worshipping golden calves. The Lord God appeared before Moses and said these beautiful and comforting words about himself:

> The LORD, the LORD, a God merciful and gracious, slow to anger, and abounding in steadfast love and faithfulness, keeping steadfast love for thousands, forgiving iniquity and transgression and sin, but who will by no means clear the guilty, visiting the iniquity of the fathers on the children and the children's children, to the third and fourth generation.[107]

Mercy, grace, and patience. Steadfast love and forgiveness. Justice.

These are the characteristics of our Creator that we need because it takes us so long to even begin to grasp his beauty and kindness. It is not simple; it is awesome, it is inspiring, and it takes much reflection to even begin to grasp just a tiny bit of the glory that is our great I AM.

TAKEAWAY 1: In order to truly know the way, we must choose to devote a part of our day to pursue and converse with God in and through the Spirit. The process of God revealing himself to us will take a lifetime and beyond. He is that awesome.

---

[107] Exodus 34:6, 7.

▪ DOUBTING YOU

Lean into your doubts; through investigation of them is found conviction and wisdom.

Of the twelve initial apostles, plus the two added later (Matthias took the place of Judas the traitor, and Saul was chosen and is known to us as Paul), only John seems to have died a natural death.

All the rest, if the traditional stories are correct, died claiming that Jesus was who he said he was, and that he died and came back from the grave.

All they likely had to do to preserve their life in the flesh was renounce those amazing claims about the Christ.

Doubting Thomas seems to have died in full conviction—doubting no more.

If you have doubts, let them out. Lean into them, and prayerfully investigate them, in the company of God's people.

You will find all honest seekers have doubts and questions. As was mentioned in an earlier chapter, we must embrace this about the Messiah: "A bruised reed he will not break, and a faintly burning wick he will not quench."[108]

Yes, the one true God is abounding in mercy, grace, and patience.

> **TAKEAWAY 2:** Lean into and investigate your doubts. Converse with God and his people; our God is merciful and encourages us in our times of doubt.

---

[108] Isaiah 42:3.

Chapter Ten

CLEANING FEET
Mary and Her Dirty Hair

MARTHA GLARED AT ME AS SHE PASSED ME IN THE DOORWAY.

I was doing it again, even though I had promised not to.

Yeshua was at our house again. Most of his closest disciples were there; my brother Lazarus was sitting next to Yeshua and John.

Everyone was listening to the teaching; I had promised Martha I wouldn't leave her hanging again, but I just couldn't stop listening. His words were so encouraging, so loving, so otherworldly.

As a woman amongst other women, I had always felt like a goat in a flock of sheep.

Martha was the pretty one—smart too. Oh, and hard-working, focused, and giving.

Other than that, she didn't have much going for her.

Lazarus, well, everyone loved him. He was outgoing, was a good judge of character, and made friends easily.

Me, well, how many times had our parents asked, "Why can't you be more like Martha?"

To be honest, I always wanted to be like her. But I couldn't be taller, prettier, more outgoing. I was a misfit. I always was fascinated by how things worked, by wisdom (I would have preferred sitting in the Temple like all the boys with the teachers to being at home, learning "women's work"). I just loved to find out why things worked, why they didn't, and to hear the stories of the people who had gone on before us. I enjoyed discussions of wisdom and philosophy.

So yeah, I wasn't much of a catch.

"Mary, Peter and Andrew are out of bread; stop daydreaming. Help me out."

She said it quietly; Yeshua had gotten on her last time she was upset with me.

Everyone but our rabbi was upset with me, pretty much for all of my life. I'm not the typical Hebrew girl. But our rabbi, our Yeshua, we hit it off from the first time we met.

I don't really know why we became fast friends; he was talking, I was listening. I asked a bunch of questions, just like I did with everyone. But he was different. He didn't seem to mind my questions; he always had this smile when I spoke, like he was looking at someone he enjoyed. It seemed like he knew me before he ever met me, and maybe I knew him too?

I had not met many people who liked me, and I really couldn't blame them.

I saw the way the boys looked at Martha before she married: like a hungry man looked at a big leg of lamb on the fire.

Me? Not so much. I was short, my hair was ratty. I didn't have that pleasing form guys just couldn't resist. I was totally resistible, apparently.

But Jesus, he just seemed to enjoy me: plain ol' me.

For the longest time, I just couldn't accept why he put up with me. Well, it was more than putting up; he sought me out. He would stop by regularly, talking to all of us, but at some point, late in the evening, we would just sit on the roof and talk. He never seemed disappointed in my lack of usefulness, skills, or attraction as a woman. He just, we just, were sort of knit together.

I finally came to accept what I had felt from everyone, except Lazarus, my entire life: I was a disappointment. I was hard to relate to. I was awkward. I wasn't very womanly.

But Jesus, he just loved me. Just because I was Mary. He didn't care that I wasn't a good cook (he was honest about preferring to fast rather than eat my bread; he was so funny), or that I was pretty short, or even that I wasn't good with children. My not being married didn't seem to matter to him; he never once asked me when I was going to get married. He did ask me if I wanted to be married (I wasn't too sure; I really wanted to be a priest and study the scrolls—pretty weird for a woman).

And about Lazarus; well, he wore me out too, up until he died. When he came back, he was, well, a whole lot more like the rabbi. It was a complete transformation. He couldn't seem to hug me or tell me how great I was often enough. But then he was different in a way that made me wonder, and he and I had some long talks, just like the ones I had with Yeshua. He shared some things about death, about how it wasn't death; it helped me to understand the rabbi.

"Mary!" Martha was getting louder. "Will you please?" She stopped. She had made eye contact with Yeshua again; he just laughed.

"Never mind, I got it." She shook her head and scurried on. She gave up; I gave up.

I sat on the floor next to the wall. Yeshua smiled and handed his food to me. "The food is good, Mary; I guess you weren't cooking tonight?" His eyes sparkled, and then we both broke out laughing.

"No, Yeshua, I wanted to make sure you would come back to see us."

He had the best laugh; he was the funniest person I had ever known. As our laughter died down, a look came to his face, one I had seen a few times lately. It was a sort of sadness. I perceived it was about that coming back thing.

He had been trying to tell us; it was just too hard to hear. But Lazarus had picked up on it while he was … well, you know, that Yeshua was really going to die. We thought his kingdom was going to be physical, and Yeshua would be like King David on the throne; that was not the plan at all. It was hard for me to grasp, hard to hear, and I couldn't see it for the longest.

But in his eyes tonight, as we looked at each other, it was becoming clearer. His kingdom was much bigger than Israel. I had asked him one beautiful night on the roof, "What will the kingdom look like?"

His response, "You know when the Father spoke through Isaiah, he said, 'For my thoughts are not your thoughts, neither are your ways my ways, declares the LORD. For as the heavens are higher than the earth, so are my ways higher than your ways and my thoughts than your thoughts.'"[109]

He kept eye contact, smiling his gentle and beautiful smile of love. He was telling me I was not thinking it through. "So, it's not really all this and Jerusalem?" I asked, motioning outward toward our village, the few lights, and looking inquisitively at him.

---

[109] Isaiah 55:8, 9.

He smiled broadly. "No, much bigger." His hands motioned toward the stars, the town, and then ... to me? "Much more beautiful." He laughed, and tears flowed from his eyes. He always showed such joy whenever I started to figure things out.

"Mary, you okay?" Yeshua's voice was tender; I'm not even sure if he said it out loud or if he was doing that thing he often did. Sometimes, his voice just happened in between my ears; it was glorious. But I looked at him, and his eyes were wet, as were mine. I guess while I thought of him, tears of mercy, gratitude, and thanks had begun to flow down my face.

"He leaving soon," I said to myself. It was true; he was going to go where Lazarus had been. I was happy for him; he deserved so much more than what he received wherever this was. I looked him over; I wanted to freeze this picture of my truest friend, the one person who seemed not only to get me but to love me for who I was. My heart suddenly overflowed with gratitude, and then I saw his feet.

They were nasty again. He had spent the day healing, feeding, talking to people, and loving them. When he came in the house, he just kept on loving people, and we all came to him with our requests. No one ever thought to wash his feet and ask him what he needed.

I looked back at his feet. The meal was almost over; everyone would probably be heading home or going to sleep soon. But my heart; he was leaving soon, and not just like our other guest. He was really leaving. For some reason, now, in this moment, I accepted it; I couldn't bear it, but Laz had told me it was good thing, a very good thing to leave this life.

I knew Yeshua was, well, he was somehow, God in the flesh. No man or woman could have been as wonderful, knowing, powerful, meek, or gentle as this man was. He was more than he seemed. He was going back? That would be so wonderful for him.

But now my tears flowed, and I began sobbing. He looked at me, and I jumped up and ran past Martha to my corner of the house. I grabbed the perfume, one of my few things of value; I had saved for a long time to have some extra provisions, but then a few months ago, after Lazarus had come back to us, I bought this. It was an impulse, but one I couldn't seem to stop. I didn't know why I spent so much on it, but now I did.

We had done the best we could with Lazarus when he died, but this perfume was excellent. I ran in and fell at Jesus's feet; the whole house went silent. I suddenly realized I had not grabbed a towel; no need. I pulled my ratty hair down, broke open the container, and began washing my friend's dirty feet. The smell of the perfume was glorious. My tears mingled with the oily liquid. I stole glances at him; he was smiling, and tears were flowing.

My dearest friend, he had to go; I just wanted to send him off properly. I had to say thank you for all those times talking on the roof, for not looking at me the way other people did, for just finding me to be more than enough reason to find joy.

"Why was this ointment not sold for three hundred denarii and given to the poor?"[110]

I recognized the voice, but I kept cleaning Yeshua's feet. The dirt was really caked on; he was a mess. I pulled my hair hard to the right and rubbed the dirt off. These wonderful feet of my truest friend would be clean and soothed.

"Leave her alone, so that she may keep it for the day of my

---

[110] John 12:5.

burial. For the poor you always have with you, but you do not always have me."[111] My friend was defending me, he always defended me. Against Judas, against Martha, against anyone; he was always looking out for me.

This? Cleaning his feet, it's all I could do.

We are friends; Laz said someday we would be with him in a place of amazing comfort and glory and I could ask all the annoying questions I wanted, and the bread was already baked (Good news for all of us, according to Lazarus).

After everyone left, I just sat on the floor for a bit. Yeshua came and pulled me to my feet.

"Beautiful stars out tonight, Mary."

We climbed up on the roof and sat; it was a glorious night. The air was clear and cool, and we sat for a long time without saying anything.

"You probably should wash your hair, Mary."

I busted out laughing. "No, I'm good."

He took my ratty, dirty hair and sort of straightened it with his hands. "It's a good look for you, pretty friend. Know you are loved, Mary." His voice was gentle and sweet.

"I know."

UNPACKING MARY AND HER HAIR

Not a lot is said about Mary and Martha. But something was different about Mary.

I would suspect, from the interaction in Luke 10:28–42,

---

[111] John 12:7, 8.

that many who knew her found her to be lacking in the expected womanly graces of her day.

After all, she was more interested in learning from Jesus than in serving food, like a good woman should, right? She had to know the social expectations and feel the pressure to do what women normally did in such situations. Young men were attached to rabbis, not the young ladies. How dare she?

I know as a young boy and on into early adulthood, I felt like a misfit. I didn't enjoy a lot of things most men did (sports, hunting, etc.), and I got a lot of strange looks from people. I was tall, lanky, and uncoordinated, and lacked social skills of any sort. I was bookish and curious. It's a lonely way to live.

I wonder about Mary; she probably did know what was expected of her as a woman in a social situation, but just couldn't consistently pull it off. Her love of learning from Jesus overruled the social expectations. Her desire to honor and show love to her friend when his feet were dirty earned her condemnation from some (likely more than just Judas; he was just rude enough to say it out loud), but her friend saw it as what is was: love.

Beautiful, over-the-top, and sacrificial love. She did what she could for the Messiah with all she had: perfume and hair.

Let's look at some lessons from Mary and her friendship with Jesus:

THE GOOD PORTION

Our "Jesus," the author and perfecter of our faith, the guarantee of our salvation, and the lover of our soul—he is eternal and fully God. His teaching is worth listening to.

Mary, Martha, and Lazarus were all good friends of Jesus. They were all very different. Yet Jesus loved each of them for who they were.

In the story of Mary and Martha, Martha was upset because Mary did not help serve the food to all the guests. She requests that Jesus straighten her out. His response: "Martha, Martha, you are anxious and troubled about many things, but one thing is necessary. Mary has chosen the good portion, which will not be taken away from her."[112]

Knowing what we know, Mary and Martha are both in the presence of God himself. He is sitting and sharing what he knows; for some reason, Mary is entranced. She is soaking it in, and as he says, this is the good portion.

It is also good to serve others, food or whatever they need. It is all a "good portion."

When we awake in the morning, let us honestly ask ourselves, "What is the best portion for this first part of my day?"

Maybe it is rolling out of the bed, grabbing a cup of coffee, and sitting in intimate friendship with the Lord.

Or perhaps it is calming a crying child or loving a spouse by offering your body to them.

Maybe it is taking breakfast to an elderly neighbor who is isolated and could use the company.

We must choose good portions, and these choices are best made by walking perceptively in the Spirit.

But at some point, if the Word of God (the Bible) is the Word of God, then we need to sit on the roof with Jesus and listen, converse, and reflect on his teachings. It is the best portion.

---

[112] Luke 10:41, 42.

> **TAKEAWAY 1:** At some point in every day, we must choose to calm ourselves and commune with Jesus in his Word, which is the whole of scripture.

BE WHO GOD MEANT YOU TO BE

If you feel like a misfit, know you are created for a purpose and you are loved. You have someone who gets you; be the you your Creator meant for you to be.

Some of us have interests that defy social expectations. Mary, I perceive, was one of these people.

Not every man loves sports and hunting. Not every woman wants to be a wife and mother. Not every child should pursue a college degree, nor should every child attend a trade school. The familiar Proverb states that a child should be trained "in the way he [or she] should go," implying that God has a path for the unique talents and abilities he implanted in each of us.

Not long after God created us in the beautiful garden, there were three men, children of Cain, and they had unique abilities:[113]

- Jabal—dwelt in tents and tended livestock
- Jubal—played the lyre and pipe (and I suppose knew how to make such musical things)
- Tubal-cain—forged bronze and iron implements

We are not, according to the Word, blank slates. God implanted within us a "way that we should go." In the intersection between the

---

[113] Genesis 4:20–22.

needs of the Kingdom of God and our abilities is our usefulness to our Lord and his Kingdom.

Mary was a "priest" of the type the New Covenant establishes. Each of us has the ability, through the Holy Spirit, to intercede and speak with the Father in prayer. No ordination is needed. We are all priests in this kingdom of the heart. The teachings of God drew and kept Mary's heart; I conjecture she was a great help to many in their spiritual growth, spending so much time listening and thinking through what Jesus taught her.

Martha had a servant's heart. She no doubt encouraged, fed, and showered many people with love.

Martha was Martha, and Mary was Mary. Yeshua loved them both.

TAKEAWAY 2: Prayerfully ask the Lord to show you who he made you to be and how that fits into his Kingdom objectives, and joyfully join him in his work. Be who he knows and loves.

Chapter Eleven

THE LONGEST SWIM

Peter Dives In

"It is the Lord,"[114] shouted John.

I stood up; I could see a man standing on the shore, maybe two hundred cubits away. I quickly pulled on my tunic, plunged into the sea, and began to swim toward him.

It had been a long and very silent night. Some of us had gathered the evening before. My wife had prepared some food; we had all picked at it, but no one had much of an appetite. It was hard; I think all of us were in the same place emotionally. We were all lost in our thoughts of our abandonment of our Lord. I was feeling very unsettled and had a gnawing sense of dread in my stomach.

Yeshua was back from the dead. His body was scarred, but he was the same smiling, loving, and encouraging person he had been before that ugly night. I was thrilled, terrified, and confused.

I had talked so big on that terrible night. He warned us he was going somewhere and we could not follow him.

I was determined; he seemed to be saying he was going

---

[114] John 21:7.

somewhere tough and we would not have the courage to follow. At least that was my perception, so I just had to let him know what was on my heart.

"Lord, why can I not follow you now? I will lay down my life for you."[115]

His words stung a bit, but I was sure of what I had said. He gave me a sad look and said gently, "Will you lay down your life for me? Truly, truly, I say to you, the rooster will not crow till you have denied me three times."[116]

I was upset; I loved Yeshua with all I was, and I knew I would fight for him; to the death, if needed.

My mind was racing and I looked up. I had only swum maybe twenty cubits; I could see the man on the shore, watching me swim toward him. I felt a sudden pang of regret that I had jumped; he wouldn't want to see me. He couldn't.

I stopped for a moment; my arms were aching from casting and hauling the nets all night, empty until the man on the shore had shouted across the water, "Children, do you have any fish?"

That was a strange thing; I had been a fisherman all my life. Who was this man calling us children? But all of us in the boat, we had just been going through the motions all night. We just needed something to do with our hands. I suppose we used to find peace, at least, just sitting in a boat on the water at night, but that night, it didn't seem to work. None of us had peace.

Nathanael was normally a talker. He kept us laughing. I kept looking at him and hoped he would bring up something to distract us, but he just kept staring at the water. I supposed they all felt what

---

[115] John 13:37.
[116] John 13:38.

I did, that they had failed Messiah when he needed us most. It was amazing he was back, living and walking; he was exactly who he was supposed to be. He fulfilled all the prophecies; we were in awe, and we were ashamed. We had blown it.

I had blown it the biggest, well, yeah, other than maybe Judas the traitor.

No one ever stuck their foot in their mouth quite like I did.

I thought for a moment about swimming back to the boat, but no, I kept going toward the man waiting on the shore. I felt fear rising in my gut, while at the same time, his words "do not be anxious"[117] also echoed through my mind in that kind tone he had spoken them in.

Yeah, but maybe I should be anxious since I abandoned, no, betrayed the Son of God?

Yep, no one so royally messes up like I do.

Another scene replayed slowly in my mind, when my words destroyed a most beautiful gift.

John, James, and I were with our Lord on a mountain, when Yeshua suddenly became gleaming and white, and two men appeared who had not walked up that mountain with us. We quickly discovered who they were; it was so dreamlike. It was Moses and Elijah.

Moses, the one who became such a friend to God that he would sit and talk with him, and his face glowed so much that it terrified those who saw him. That Moses.

It was clear that Yeshua and Moses were close friends; they were talking just like John and I often did.

There also was the great prophet Elijah, who had stood alone,

---

[117] Matthew 6:25.

seemingly, against the four hundred prophets of Baal. Yep, friends with my friend Yeshua, just talking like good friends do.

Anyway, I was in awe, super-excited, and I spoke. I seems like I never learn not to speak; why do I always just blurt things out? But I did: "Lord, it is good that we are here. If you wish, I will make three tents here, one for you and one for Moses and one for Elijah."

It was such an amazing moment, and I was seeing Jesus as he truly was in his essence, but I didn't want the moment to end. I thought I would build little tabernacles so Jesus, Elijah, and Moses could be comfortable, and we could sit and listen to them. I wanted that moment to last.

What happened next, well, a voice came from the heavens like a rushing and powerful wind, terrifying, grand, and otherworldly; it told me, "This is my beloved son, with whom I am well pleased; listen to him."

The suddenness of it, the feeling of absolute power: The three of us non-shiny ones hit the ground flat on our faces. I thought I would die. I pushed my face into the rocky ground.

"Rise, and have no fear," I heard the kind voice of my Yeshua say. His hand touched me, and I slowly looked up, ashamed, but was met by his beautiful, smiling, and accepting face.

Far from looking condemning, he seemed amused at me.

That was so him, and so unlike every person I had ever known. I just kept messing things up; he never seemed surprised or even disappointed. He would so often just put his arm around me and give me a big squeeze. I sensed he was saying, "Hey kid, when you're ready, we'll work on that controlling nature of yours."

But still, in that moment, I felt my mouth had shortened such a glorious moment. If I had only shut my mouth and just listened.

Just like the Father said.

I swam a little more slowly now toward my friend. Or perhaps my former friend? I looked up; I wasn't making much progress toward the shore. Yes, my arms were hurting, but my heart felt like it would explode. No one messes up like I do. No one.

The man waited and watched me; I couldn't quite make out the look on his face. It was still a long swim. I looked back; the boys were still struggling to get the nets loaded with fish back into the boat.

That was the kicker on this night, after the man called us "children." We had caught nothing, I mean not even a turtle or a water-logged branch, in that long night of dragging the nets. But no one seemed frustrated; we just needed to do something. We were pretty much done by the time the man showed up on the shore, but after his first call, he then said, "Cast the net on the right side of the boat, and you will find some."[118] We just mindlessly threw our nets back out. What else were we going to do?

It was strange; I supposed I hoped it was him, but part of me hoped it wasn't. I felt maybe like a husband who had cheated on his wife would, right after she found out. As much as I wanted to be right back where I had been with him, one of his right-hand men, there's no way he would take me back again. I had messed up too big this time.

But when the man told us to throw our net to the right side, yeah, it brought up that moment when I said something that was right, just a few years ago.

It was the first time the rabbi stepped into my life in a big way.

In fact, he had stepped right into my boat. He was teaching a big crowd on the shore; me and the boys had just had a worthless night

---

[118] John 21:6.

on the lake and were drying our nets and sort of eavesdropping on the rabbi. His teaching, in spite of my mental tiredness and aching muscles, began stirring something in my heart. I was living a hard life, trying to be more successful for my wife, trying to get a little extra to live on, but things were just hard. He seemed to have a different concept of what life should be about. I found myself fully awake, listening to him eagerly and secretly wishing I could just be with him and learn a better way. His way.

That was when he turned toward us, came over, stepped right into my boat, and asked us to put out into the water a short way. As we rowed, he looked at me and arched his eyebrows, as if to say, "So this is what you wanted, right?"

I think he had this in mind all along, finding me. But what a disappointment I turned out to be. He was wrong about me.

When it was over, he looked straight at me and said, "Put out into the deep and let down your nets for a catch."[119] I remember so well what was going on inside my head: *What? What do you know about fishing? Go into the deep? We'd been fishing all night; my body ached, and I was so tired I could hardly bear the thought of throwing the nets one more time, much less dragging them in, wet and empty.*

"Master, we toiled all night and took nothing."[120]

I looked at him and hoped he would see the error of his ways; he was a great teacher, and his words hit me hard even though I was tired, but I was hoping he would at least realize that I knew fishing.

He stared at me, a kind smile on his face, and then nodded toward the deep and sat down. He just sat down. He made that face at me again, that "This is what you wanted, right?" sort of look.

---

[119] Luke 5:4.
[120] Luke 5:5.

I grabbed my oars and started rowing.

"But at your word I will let down the nets,"[121] I heard myself say, not very enthusiastically. We rowed out into the deep; he seemed to be just relaxing and enjoying the morning on the lake. I caught him looking at me several times, with an intent, a desire, to do something with me; for me?

One of those times I looked, he winked and motioned with his head, so I put down my oar and grabbed the net with one of the boys, and we threw it over the side. I started lowering myself back to sit and wait for a whole lot of nothing, just like it had been all night, when I was knocked off balance as the boat heeled over sharply, and I fell face first into the boat. The nets were suddenly pulling under our little boat. I jumped to my feet, along with the other two, and we began trying to pull the nets in.

Andrew yelled to the guys in the other boat, and they came and joined in the fight. Our boat was taking on water, but we finally got all the fish we could onboard. Both boats were full of fish and water; we barely made it to shore, rowing with all we had.

I had never seen, I had never felt—I looked at the rabbi. He was laughing. He looked at me and raised an eyebrow, again. I seemed to hear his voice inside my head, saying, "Do you want more than this?"

I looked back at the fish; the quantity was beyond what was naturally possible. The guys were exhausted and exhilarated. Jesus was just laughing. He sat there holding his sides, just taking it all in. Our eyes locked, for a moment; I sensed something was very true of him. I fell at his feet and cried out, "Depart from me, for I am a sinful man, O Lord."

---

[121] Ibid.

He probably wished he had departed from me then.

I looked toward the shore again; he was building a fire or something. What was he up to? What would he say to me when I got there? What would I, what could I say to him? I mused about just opening my mouth and drowning where I was. I couldn't face him. Me and my big mouth. Why couldn't I restrain my mouth?

But then again, why had he stopped me the other night?

That dark night, when Judas led the mob to him. I was determined that I would keep my word, I would die before I let them harm him. Our Messiah would ascend to the throne.

Judah was in bad shape; the Romans, assisted by some of our own people, were bleeding us dry. Yeshua was the promised one, the anointed, like David. He would fix all of this mess with our occupiers; we would be a strong nation once again.

But that night, when I drew my sword, I was going to defend. I was going where he was going, no matter how tough it was. We as a nation would once again determine our own destiny, and there would be a return to righteousness.

I started swinging and advancing toward the men who were intent on taking my future King, but right after the first blood was drawn, his hand was upon me again, restraining my arm holding the now bloody sword. "Put your sword into its sheath; shall I not drink the cup that the Father has given me?"[122]

In this sudden moment of violence, Jesus stepped in. Other men had stepped toward me with swords drawn, the man I had struck, he was screaming and holding the side of his head; Jesus continued holding my shaking arm and reached down, picked up a bloody ... ear?

---

[122] John 18:11.

I had swung at the man's neck; he was quick and had ducked, and I had sliced off his ear.

Jesus then motioned to those coming toward me, and they stopped, watching the man they came to take, now holding a bloody ear. He let go of my arm, took the screaming man's face in his free hand, and gently brought the severed ear to the place where it had once been. He gently moved the man's hand away; the man stopped screaming, and suddenly, save for the bloodstains, the man was whole again.

Jesus held his face for a brief moment and smiled at him gently, though there was a sadness in his eyes. The soldiers and officers of the temple slowly lowered their weapons, and for a moment, there was quiet. There was, it seemed, a complete calm in the awe of what we had just witnessed. Another miracle.

Jesus then nodded to the captain; he slowly came over and grabbed him, and the group quietly walked away.

I had been ready to die for him, but now, I perceived, I had misunderstood who he was and what he was going to do. You cannot rule from a throne in Jerusalem if you're dead, right?

I felt the bottom of the lake as I moved closer to the shore, and I stood up. There he was, sitting by the fire he had built, cooking something. He turned to me; I quickly looked down at the water. Who was he? What was this kingdom of heaven he had spoken of? Was it not to be the kingdom we had thought?

I stood, dripping, for a long while, slowly walking onto the beach. I looked back; the boys were rowing hard toward the shore, eager to see Yeshua. He had bread and fish ready, and he threw onto the fire some of our huge catch, well, the one he had caused. We ate together; I hung toward the back. I took brief glimpses of him; he seemed to be eyeing me every time.

What did he want from me? I had proven I could not be relied on.

For once in my life, I kept my mouth shut.

I always had wanted to be a leader, to have men look up to me, to be important and respected. I now had a strong desire to be invisible, unknown, and gone. I quietly resolved to spend the rest of my days quietly fishing. I didn't deserve to be his disciple. I didn't deserve the love of my wife or the admiration of anyone. My failure, it was one I could never overcome.

"Simon," his voice called out.

My heart sank; I sat and stared at the ground between my legs.

"Simon, son of John, do you love me more than these?"[123]

Why hadn't I drowned myself when I could? I continued to stare at the ground, but I just knew everyone was now looking at me. These men, these friends, who I had desired to have look at me with respect now saw me in my deep shame and failure. They were seeing, oh, God, the real Simon Peter.

Do I love him more than these? Why even ask that question? It was clear my love had failed, in spite of my big-mouthed promise that I would be the one guy to demonstrate unfailing devotion. He was asking if I loved him with an unfailing, enduring, and faithful love.

I could not talk my way out of what I had demonstrated I was incapable of, but I said, "Yes, Lord, you know that I love you."

I answered with the word for "love" that showed I loved him like a brother. I could not claim to have an unfailing and sacrificial love; I could not. Yes, I loved him, but in no way could I—

"Feed my lambs," I heard him say softly.

What, feed your—? I felt sick in my stomach; why would he say

---

[123] John 21:15.

that? He doesn't have any— Oh, does he mean … he is speaking of his—

"Simon, son of John," came his voice again, grabbing my attention from my swirling thoughts; that "son of John" thing woke me up. "Do you love me?"

I stole a glance at him now; his eyes were kind, but tears were streaming down his face. The others, the others were not looking at me, as I had supposed; they too were looking downward. I could hear soft crying all around me; what did he want from me, from us?

And it was that word again; I had told him, yes, I love you like a brother, but this was the stronger word again. I was suddenly overwhelmed; did I really love him? Could I? I began sobbing uncontrollably. I raised my head again and looked at his tear-streaked face, and I quietly choked out the words again, "Yes, Lord; you *know* that I … *love* you."[124]

"Tend my sheep."[125]

Tend your sheep? Why would he want me, of all people, to care for his sheep? Why did he use these words with the weakest and most despicable person in the group? Pick John or someone worthier.

"Simon, son of John, do you *love me like a brother*?"[126]

I felt as though he had driven a stake through my heart. I had been playing a word game with him, and he called me on it. I wouldn't dare claim to love him absolutely, so how about like a brother?

But would I have abandoned my brother like I abandoned him? But I was ready to die, for who I mistakenly believed him to be.

---

[124] John 21:16.

[125] Ibid.

[126] Ibid., v. 17; this time, Jesus uses the *phileo* form that Peter has been answering with, so I modified the translation to reflect this.

"Lord, you know *everything; you know that I love you*."[127] It was all I had. He knew me better than I knew myself.

"Feed my sheep. Truly, truly, I say to you, when you were young, you used to dress yourself and walk wherever you wanted, but when you are old, you will stretch out your hands, and another will dress you and carry you where you do not want to go."[128]

I looked up again, our eyes met. His face was gentle, and he nodded slightly. He was accepting me again?

It was like that early moment in the boat, after the first great catch. It was that look again, when he raised his eyebrow and I heard his voice in my head saying, "Do you want more?"

He was now offering me everything and more. His kingdom, it was the ultimate kingdom. This was what he had been trying to tell us all along; he had come to all people now, not to make some huge nation to defeat the Romans or any other earthly kingdom. His was the kingdom of the spirit. It was the real thing, not just the—wow, my mind was racing.

We were still locked onto one another, and his voice was firm and strong in my head.

"Rock," his name for me, "you are loved. Love these for me, now."

I smiled weakly at him; he returned the smile.

I was his now, and as he had said, I was no longer in control. I would someday be led away as he was.

That was fine.

That was a long swim back. That was a baptism of an interminable length.

---

[127] Ibid.
[128] Ibid., v. 17, 18.

But now, it was becoming clear.

I was loved. I had a heart full of him.

I would now cut loose and share that overflowing love.

I could no longer care about me, for he was now abiding in me. He could no longer be contained. Love was the path, unfailing, abiding, joy-filled love from him and for him and to him.

UNPACKING PETER AND THE LONGEST SWIM

I ran into a precious believing friend of mine; we had not seen each other in a while. After a moment of catching up, she cautiously asked, "Did you hear about me and …?" and mentioned the name of her former husband, another good friend of mine from the past.

I had heard of their divorce. What she said, I suppose many of us have felt this way about something in our life, just as Peter was shocked at his own failure: "I never thought I would be the one getting divorced. I taught women's classes [at church] and told these women that we stay married. I never thought I would be one who didn't."

The experience of Peter and his denial of the Christ is not uncommon; probably most of us have done it at some level. Let's look at a few lessons from this story:

WHEN YOU TAKE A HIT, KEEP FIGHTING

As much as we may love God, we are living in a "body of death,"[129] as the apostle Paul put it; our flesh and our trained responses to pain and difficulty sometimes get the best of us. When we take a

---

129 Romans 7:24.

hit in our spiritual warfare, we must endeavor, as Peter did, to get up, let God and our loving church family dress our wounds, and get right back in the fight.

All of us sin and fall short of the glory of God,[130] and as was mentioned in an earlier chapter, when God delivered the law, he also included the provision for atonement for those moments when we would break that same law. We need our Lord, always.

The wrong response to failure (sin) is to curl up in a ball and suck our thumbs. Jesus left the earth shortly after this seaside breakfast of fish and bread; Peter and the other apostles are found standing for God shortly thereafter. Peter and John end up in trouble with the council in Jerusalem and passed that test with flying colors.

They stood firm.

If you have big sin in your life, get those wounds dressed (spend time with God and his people), and get back in the fight. Satan only wins if you stop standing.

> **TAKEAWAY 1:** Peter's example of betrayal should remind us that we are in a pitched spiritual battle; the victory belongs not to us but to him who abides in us. When you fail, struggle with the help of the Spirit and God's people back to your feet and keep marching on. We have the victory through Christ; the final sacrifice has been made. Do not give up.

---

[130] Ibid., 3:23.

It is natural to think of our failures to stand for Jesus in human terms. Once again, we are of the supernatural; Jesus invites us to "feed his sheep," even after a massive failure.

We learn from an early age that most human relationships carry an element of transaction in them. You clean up your room, your mom is happy and lets you have pie. We do nice for people who do nice for us; we often extract a pound of flesh from those who let us down.

That is not the way of the Christ.

According to Paul in his letter to the church of Ephesus, "In him we have *redemption* through his blood, according to the *riches* of his grace, which he *lavished* upon us."[131]

Each of us who wears his name must embrace this truth: When Yeshua lavishes us with grace, it is very lavish.

We will, at times, give in to our body of death. But we must always choose to believe that what he did on the cross was more than enough.

Stand in his grace, and see his power work for good through you.

TAKEAWAY 2: Stop being transactional in your relationship with others. God is not transactional with you. Lavish the grace he has lavished upon you onto others.

---

[131] Ephesians 1:7, 8.

Chapter Twelve

ABIDING IN CHRIST, CHRIST ABIDING IN YOU

Shalom

YES, JESUS DID TELL HIS DISCIPLES A VERY HARD THING WHEN he was approaching his Crucifixion:

> Yet a little while and the world will see me no more, but you will see me. Because I live, you also will live. In that day you will know that I am in my Father, and you in me, and I in you. Whoever has my commandments and keeps them, he it is who will be loved by my Father, and I will love him and manifest myself to him.[132]

I hope you found joy and encouragement in seeing Jesus through these fictional stories based on those who walked with our Lord. I pray that your zeal and love for Yeshua the Christ has

---

[132] John 14:19–21.

grown. May your desire to see him more fully by devouring the Word of God increase. I hope that as Jesus said above, in spite of the fact the world does not see him, you see him more vividly than ever.

We are called to an impossible mission: to change the hearts of the lost and sinful people around us, people living in conflict, fear, confusion, addiction, and stress. When the angelic hosts proclaimed, "Peace among those with whom he is pleased," do the lost of the world see that peace in you? Our neighbors need peace and hope; do they find that in you?

It is not the case that Jesus came to establish an earthly kingdom, a utopian world in which everyone is full of love and joy.

It is the case that we who have Christ in us show to the world a peace that surpasses understanding.[133] My prayer is that this simple book will inspire you to dwell in the Word daily, to see the beauty of the Lord, to recognize his voice and his hand, and to walk with him in love as you keep his commands, which are not, as he said, burdensome.

What are his commands?

Love God, love your neighbor.

May the Messiah be manifest in you with power, and may you do his work of love wherever he has placed you in life. May you be bold and full of grace, as the love of Christ that overflows in you splashes onto those around you.

Shalom to you, my friend; may Christ dwell in you, and you in him.

---

[133] Philippians 4:7.

Milton Keynes UK
Ingram Content Group UK Ltd.
UKHW041833280823
427655UK00012B/251/J